DEMYSTIFYING BRA FITTING AND CONSTRUCTION

BY NORMA LOEHR

To my husband for his unwavering support

TABLE OF CONTENTS

MEASURING FOR BRA SIZE

PATTERNS

TESTING AND THE TOILE

FITTING

TECHNIQUES

FOREWORD

Whenever I tell someone I am a bra maker, I am regarded with equal amounts of curiosity and be-fuddlement. I don't know where people think bras come from but clearly few have considered the possibility of actually making them. I regularly meet women who are in the midst of creating couture garments and are frankly intimidated to go near a bra making project.

Initially, I felt the same way. When I started making bras several years ago, I aggressively searched for and collected everything I could find on the topic. I found precious little. Making bras seemed to be some sort of closely guarded black art. Bra makers seem to jealously guard their secrets, as if it fell into the wrong hands it would be used for evil like Harry Potter magic or The Force.

It took extended study with a bra making pro, followed by some serious time practicing on friends and family before I had achieved mastery of the craft and accepted custom commissions from clients. In the end, I learned the most — and continue to learn the most - by doing, repeatedly.

I believe that every woman who sews should be making her own bras. What we wear underneath our clothing is the foundation for all the other lovely garments we spend hours carefully crafting. All in all, a bra will take just a few hours to make and it is something you will certainly wear. This book will tell you exactly how to fit and construct your own professional looking bra.

INTRODUCTION

My goal is to give seamstresses the necessary knowledge and confidence to sew their own bras by demystifying fitting and the construction techniques to get professional looking results.

Rather than attempt to cover the seemingly limitless variations of bra styles and fabrication techniques, I focus on the most common bra making techniques that I use daily in my workroom to get consistently beautiful results.

My techniques are independent of a specific bra pattern. While I suggest what to look for when selecting a bra pattern, this book does not provide one, nor are there instructions for drafting and grading bra patterns. You are free to work with any pattern you wish or draft your own.

No book on bra making would be complete without addressing fitting. Because I have to fit a wide variety of body types and have limited scheduled time with my clients, I developed a systematic fitting process to quickly achieve a fitted toile (a.k.a. "muslin"). I provide instructions on how to work through this process and how to solve the most common fitting challenges you will encounter.

Finally, I assume that you know how to sew, have the level of experience where you know how to make pattern alterations, and can sew a collared button down shirt on your own. If you are a beginner, there is nothing stopping you from using this book to make a bra, but you may need a good sewing fundamentals book to help you through. I have a list of suggested sewing reference books at http://www.orange-lingerie.com/resources.

If there are bra making topics you want to learn about, send me an email at info@orange-lingerie.com. If there are enough inquires, I will write a blog post in response or perhaps even another book!

SEW YOUR OWN

Need some reasons to sew your own bras? How about 10 of them?

1. It is actually cheaper than buying a bra.

Surprise! Once you have the pattern, all the materials - fabric, findings and trims - can cost as little as $15. Of course you can also spend a lot more too! Regardless of what you spend on materials, the quality of the bra you make yourself will far surpass the one from the store.

2. It is faster and more efficient than shopping for a bra.

With experience, it will only take a few hours from tracing the pattern to wearing the completed bra. Compare this to the time it takes you to get to the store, park, find the bras you like, try them on, pay, etc. Even finding bras online can take some serious time, especially once you factor in the returns and exchanges as you try to find the ones that fit.

3. You get what exactly you want.

You get to choose the color, fabric, trim, etc. You could, if you were so inclined, make a bra for each outfit. That plunging top? That racer back tank? That sheer blouse? No problem. You have a bra for that.

4. You get a bra that fits.

With no real size standardization for ready-to-wear bras, your best hope for a bra that fits is to make your own (or have one made for you). Plus, once you have a pattern that fits, you can replicate it time and time again without worrying about the bra being discontinued, sold out or no longer available. Since bras must be regularly replaced, this is a big deal.

5. It will be easier to fit the other garments you are sewing.

You will find fewer alterations are necessary to the bodice of your garment when your bust is contained and positioned correctly on your body, due to a bra that fits you properly.

6. You will become a better seamstress.

There are plenty of construction techniques in a bra making project to help you refine your skills. We can all benefit from practicing precision ¼" seaming and parallel lines of topstitching. The best part is that no one else but you (well almost no one!) will see any of those microscopic sewing "imperfections".

7. You can regain your sewing momentum.

There is nothing like a high utility project that can be completed in a few hours to get you back into sewing. Bras are a perfect sewing jumpstart when you are stalled on other more complicated projects.

8. You can replicate your favorite bra.

We have all been there. You love it, it fits, but it must be retired. You search and cannot find one anywhere. Copy it. You can also improve on the fit in the duplication process.

9. You've just found a way to use your sewing machine's embroidery and embellishment features.

All those decorative stitches that you have not used since you bought your machine can be put to work. Astonishingly, with today's embroidery-enabled machines, you can even make your own lace.

10. You become a better judge of quality materials and craftsmanship and know when to pay for it.

There you have it -ten great reasons to sew your own bras. Time to get sewing!

BASIC BRA ANATOMY

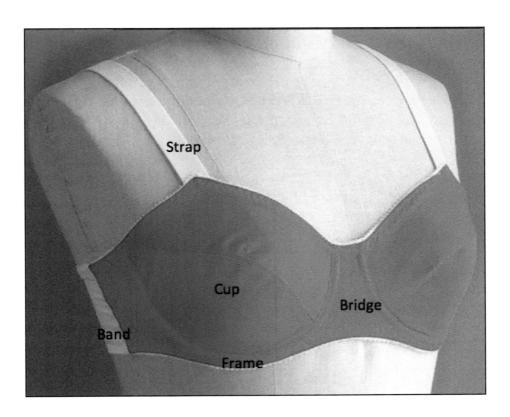

Before we talk about making bras, I want to establish a common vocabulary for talking about the different parts of a bra. It's not that we don't know what a bra is, but rather that most of us have never really examined a bra in order to understand what they are made of and how they work. While some of the parts of the bra and their function are obvious (the cups contain the breasts), others are not (the band supports the cups, not the straps). To demystify the bra itself, what follows is an overview of its components and their respective functions.

CUPS

The cups are the part of the bra that holds the breasts. The most obvious role of the cups is to contain and support the breasts. To do this, the cups must harness the breast tissue into one place and direct it all where we want it to go — forward and up, defying gravity.

BAND

The band refers to the part of the bra that wraps around your body. It may be news to you that the band, not the straps, is primarily responsible for supporting the cups.

Unlikely as it sounds, consider this: underneath the cups (so underneath your breasts) are wires (the underwires). The wires take the pressure of the breasts in the cups and spread it out over their entire length and their surroundings, primarily into the band. If the band is insufficiently wide for your size (e.g. too narrow under the arm and around the back), you will not get the necessary support from your bra since there is not enough surface area in the band to absorb the wire transfer of pressure from the cups.

You may wonder about bras without underwires. Admittedly, it is possible to get some breast support from a bra that does not have underwires, but not nearly as much as wired bras, and the band must be quite wide in order to do so. Of course, if you don't plan on wearing the bra for an extended period of time or are not wearing a bra for support, you can skip the wires. The other wire exceptions are women who are nursing or who just had surgery to the area.

BRIDGE

The bridge of the bra is the center front area between the cups. The bridge provides separation of the breasts, putting the breasts in proper position to ease into the cups. If the bridge does not match the spacing between your breasts, the bra will not sit flat against your body. The bridges in store-bought bras rarely match up with an individual's breast spacing.

FRAME

The frame is the cup holder of the bra. Surprisingly, frames are actually optional! For frameless bras, the cups are joined directly to the band and to the bridge. So long as they are well designed and constructed, frameless and full frame bras will provide equivalent support. Please note that you cannot simply omit the frame from a full frame pattern and get the same results.

STRAPS

It varies by style but generally the straps of the bra extend from the top corner of the bra cup, go up and over the shoulder, and join to the back of the bra. If your shoulders show strap marks that implies the straps are supporting the cups, and that is not how it is supposed to be! The role of the straps is to hold the bra cups and band in the proper position on the body. If the bra is strapless, the band must be built to hold itself in the correct position on the body.

Now that we have a common vocabulary for discussing bras, you will learn about how these parts fit together on your body in the next section: How a Bra Should Fit.

HOW A BRA SHOULD FIT

Fit may be one of the things that got you interested in making bras in the first place. It certainly was the driver for me. We all know what a great fitting bra feels like: the best ones are like an extension of your body, almost weightless, and unnoticeable. We all want that!

But how should a bra fit? It is actually a combination of things. At its simplest, the best fitting bra completely encapsulates the breast tissue, bringing it out from under the arm and off the rib cage so the breasts are lifted to a front facing position. It does all of this while lying flat against the body with no wrinkles or ripples - in the bra or on the body.

For a bra to achieve perfect fit as a whole, each part of the bra must do its job. So let's take a look at each part of the bra and how it should fit.

CUPS

The cups fully enclose the breast tissue and provide the desired contours. While there are varying degrees of coverage possibilities on the top of the breast, the bottom portion of the cup must contain the breast entirely.

If the cups are too large, the breasts are not fully supported and will sag into the open spaces and the bra will look baggy. While this may be comfortable, the constant pull of gravity on the tissue surrounding the breasts can lead to an unattractive future, not to mention what this does to the body's current profile. And there's more bad news: ill fitting cups can also allow the apex of the breast to point outward rather than straight ahead. Since this creates an illusion of width, it is also unattractive.

If the cups are too small, in addition to discomfort, the bra will not lie flat on the body. It will be rippled and the wearer's body may be as well, as it squeezes out from underneath the bra.

BRIDGE

The bridge spans the space between the breasts, lying flat against the body and putting the cups and underwires in precise position to hold and support the breasts. If the bridge is too wide, the cups are too far apart and the bra will stand away from the body, creating a sort of uni-cup that does not hold or support the breasts effectively. On the other hand, if the bridge is too small, the breasts are pinched together.

BAND

From reading the section on Basic Bra Anatomy, you know that the band of a bra is key to supporting the breasts. If the band is not wide enough to handle the pressure from supporting the breasts, there are two ill effects. The first effect is that the support job will be transferred to the straps, which can cause shoulder pain, as well as dig the straps into the skin. The second effect is that the torso will bulge out over the top of the band (the infamous "back fat"), which no one wants.

The bra band should not be too tight or too loose but it should be snug. If the band is too loose, the bra can move around which usually means the breasts pull the back of the band up as they sag down in front. A band that is too tight will be uncomfortable and will pull the entire bra too tightly against the body causing the body to protrude around the bra. That's not the look we are going for.

How tight is tight enough? I use a "two finger" rule. That is, only two fingers should fit under the back of the band when the bra is fastened at its loosest or middle row of hooks.

UNDERWIRES

The underwires sit directly under the breasts against the body and match the diameter of the breasts. This fit allows the wires to do their job of spreading the stress of breast support into the band. If wires are too small, they will dig into the breast tissue. If they are too large, they will dig into the body. If the wires don't fit correctly, they can also shift and twist. As you can imagine, or perhaps you know from personal experience, ill-fitting wires make for a long uncomfortable day.

STRAPS

Ideally bra straps should extend in a line from just outside the apex of the breast toward the mid point of the shoulder, however, many women prefer to wear their straps further out on the shoulder. So long as the back band is parallel to the floor and the bra cups are at the correct height for the wearer, this is not a problem.

As I mentioned in the prior section, straps don't support the breasts — they just maintain the position of the band and cups on the body. Straps should not slide, move around or dig in to the shoulder or anywhere else. You should barely notice they are there.

MORE GOOD REASONS FOR A GOOD FIT

Of course we want bras to fit comfortably, but there are other benefits too. Clothes fit better with the proper bra. If your breasts are not properly positioned on the body, the silhouette of your garments will not match the intention of the designer. You will have fullness and flatness in unintended areas, distorting the fit and drape of your clothing. By making a bra that fits you properly, issues of fit for dresses, shirts and jackets will decrease or even completely disappear!

Then, there is the slimming benefit. A properly fitting bra makes you look thinner. An ill-fitting bra allows the breasts to ride too low, thus hiding the torso and waist. A fitted bra raises the breasts revealing the torso. Slimming occurs in another dimension as well: a fitted bra directs the breast tissue out from under the arms to a forward facing position on the body. This makes you look smaller, as this decreases bulk along the side of your body.

PUTTING YOUR BRA ON

It might seem obvious how to put a bra on your body, but I found that many of my clients were not completing the process of getting the bra positioned on their body. To get the full benefit of support and lift from your bra, there are some important steps in putting the bra on your body.

There are two main ways to put on a bra with back hooks. One is to hook the bra in front and swivel the bra around so the hooks go to the back, and then put your arms through the straps as you position the cups. The second is to put your arms through the bra straps and reach behind your back to hook the bra closed then adjust the cups into position. Whichever of these methods you choose does not matter. The only caveat is that if you do swivel the bra around to the back, do not do so aggressively. Yanking on the bra could bend the underwires and will most certainly decrease the life of the elastics.

Getting the bra onto the body is only part of the equation. You also need to position the breast tissue into the cups and get the underwire into position. To get the breast tissue into the cups, lean forward and reach into a cup with your opposite hand and scoop the breast tissue out from the underarm into the bra cup. Next, place the underwire where it should be — right around the breast tissue at the chest wall. Many women skip these two steps, and by doing so are skipping out on the full shaping and support benefits of their bra.

Now that the cups are positioned correctly, take note of the straps. The straps should secure the bra in the correct horizontal position on the body without digging into your shoulder. You may need to shorten or lengthen them via the rings and sliders. I recommend taking the bra off to adjust the straps, as it's much easier that way. Before you take the bra off to adjust it, try to estimate the necessary increase or decrease. Exact measurement is futile. It may take more than one adjustment and fitting to get the length just right.

BRA CARE AND MAINTENANCE

If you want your bras to perform at their best and last as long as possible, you need to wash your bra after wearing it once, or maximally twice. Think about it: the bra is worn directly against your body so it collects body oils and skin cells. Elastic, a key component of the bra band and straps, does not respond well to either substance. When these materials get into the elastic, its ability to stretch and contract is decreased. It takes a proper wash to remove these substances so the elastic can go back to doing its job. If you wear your bras twice before washing, you need to give the bra a day off in between wearings. The elastic needs time to recover and go back to a neutral position.

So, how do you wash a bra? Let's start with what you do not do: do not put your bra in the washing machine. I know you want to because it is so easy. Do not do it! Remember there are wires encased under each bra cup. Those wires do important support work in your bra. They need to keep their shape and stay right where they are. In the washer (yes, even in the delicate cycle), the water pressure and the pressure of clothing around the bra (even in the lingerie bag) could cause the wire to twist and lose its shape. Think about your other clothes too. Those bra hooks can catch on whatever else you have in the washer or the lingerie bag (even if you fasten them before you put them in the wash).

What about the dryer, you ask? I'll be blunt: the dryer will ruin the elastic. I don't care what temperature you use. Elastic is key to the bra's function, and, as outlined above, elastic needs to be cared for properly.

All of this means one thing: hand washing and air-drying are key to cleaning the bra. To wash a bra, use lukewarm water and a gentle detergent. Gentle is the operative word. I like Eucalan since they sell handy travel packets. You can find more gentle cleanser ideas at http://www.orange-lingerie.com/resources.

Let the bras (separated by color, of course) soak for approximately 30 minutes to allow the soap and water to work their cleaning magic.

Rinse the soap from the bras in lukewarm water. To gently extract the excess water from a bra without squeezing it, lay the bra inside a towel and gently press down on the towel. Then lay the bra on a towel to dry. This soak-and-press technique is actually quite easy and does not require much active time at all.

If you follow these care instructions, a high quality bra that is worn twice a week will last between six and nine months. Regardless of care, there will come a time when a wash will not be able to resurrect the bra's elastic and that is when the bra's useful life is over.

EQUIPMENT AND SUPPLIES
FOR BRA MAKING

If you are sewing, and I assume you are, you already have many of the supplies necessary to sew a bra. In this section I provide information on the attributes of the different tools used for sewing bras and how you will be using them. Where applicable I provide specific recommendations for bra making. You can find a concise list of the equipment I use at http://www.orange-lingerie.com/resources.

I will say this numerous times, but it is important that you select the best tools for your fabric and test them on your fabric before using them on your project.

MACHINERY

Sewing machine

Your sewing machine needs for bra making are simple: straight stitch, zigzag and 3-step zigzag stitches are all that you absolutely need. You will appreciate features such as a moveable needle position, a ¼" stitch setting and a memory to preserve your favorite settings for the different parts of the construction process. While the extras are certainly nice to have, they are not necessary.

You can also make life easier by using special presser feet, such as the edge joining foot for topstitching and a zipper foot for sewing straps and the back fasteners. Other specialty machine attachments may come in to play, depending on your design choices, such as the binding attachment foot or feet for special embellishments or an embroidery hoop. Of course, these attachments are optional.

NEEDLES & THREAD

Sewing Machine Needles

Generally, I use knit fabrics with some give or stretch, so I use Stretch needles for general bra construction. The Stretch needle is designed to prevent skipped stitches in elastic materials. I replace the needle after every other bra since sewing elastics really takes its toll on the needle.

When sewing topstitching and closing underwire casing, a Universal sharp needle is recommended. You need the sharpness of that needle to get through all the layers. I also use a Universal if I am working with clear elastic.

Hand Sewing Needles

Hand sewing needles are only necessary if you want to add a bow or other embellishment to the center front. Every other part of the bra is sewn by machine.

Pins

I generally use knit fabrics for bras, so when I need pins I reach for the glass head ballpoint variety. Ballpoint pins are designed to go through the fibers of the cloth without cutting them, preventing snags and runs. Depending on your fabric, you could also use glass head ultra fine head pins.

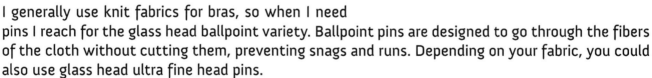

Pro tip: Keep a separate disposal container for sharp objects like broken needles and damaged pins. If they are loose in the trash they can harm animals, children and even you.

Thread

Bras need to have strong seams that can hold up under repeated pressure. To sew bras I use a fine 100% Polyester thread that does not leave any trace of fuzziness. For basting, you may want to use a thread that breaks more easily, such as a lightweight cotton thread for easy removal from the fabric.

CUTTING

Scissors

You need quality shears to cut fabric, elastics, etc. I recommend serrated shears since the serrated blade slightly grips fabric, so there is no slipping in the cutting process.

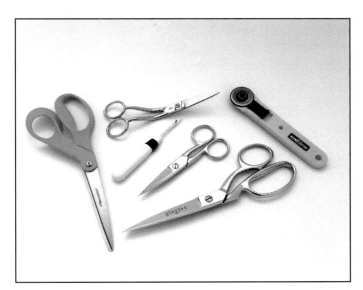

For clipping threads and notches, I like small knife-edge tailor's scissors and for trimming seams, I use offset scissors. You can also use duck-billed scissors if you are more comfortable with them.

For cutting paper, you need a separate pair of scissors because you should never use your fabric shears on paper. Any paper scissors will work for the task.

Rotary Cutter and Self Healing Mat

These are great tools for cutting strips of stabilizer and straps accurately and quickly. I like the 45mm size for cutting straps and stabilizer strips. If you want to use one to cut our your pattern, use the smaller 28mm size cutter. Note that you will need to change rotary cutter blades frequently to avoid any accidental fabric snags.

Paper and Pattern Weights

You can use any smooth weighted object that is small enough to stay inside the pattern pieces for this purpose. Whatever you use, be sure it is heavy enough to keep everything in place while you work and is smooth with no rough edges that can get caught on your fabric.

Seam ripper

A seam ripper is a necessary tool for those inevitable times when you need to fix a mistake. I also use a seam ripper to harvest the usable hardware from old bras.

MEASURING AND MARKING

Measuring tape

You will use a measuring tape to obtain your bra size as described in the Measuring for Bra Size section. I recommend you select one that is marked in ⅛" increments and ideally includes metric measurements as well. The metric system allows you to use smaller increments of measurement for precision.

Ruler

Use a ruler that you can see through with markings every $\frac{1}{16}$" like the C-Thru B85. I like to have a few of these lying around since they are used extensively in the pattern making and alteration process. I use one that is 12" long since it is easier to move around the table and small bra pattern pieces.

French Curve

While any French curve will work, look for nice rounded shapes like those you see in lingerie and clothing. You will use this to trace and alter your pattern pieces.

Measuring gauge

A ruler with a sliding gauge will help you measure for symmetry on each side of the bra throughout the construction process. I prefer a metric gauge for finer measurements.

Fabric Marker

You will need a removable marking tool to indicate important match points on your fabric. You MUST test your marker on a scrap of fabric before using it to be absolutely sure the marking can be completely removed. The ability to remove markings depends on the fabric and you don't want to complete the bra only to have the construction markings remain visible. My marker choice varies with my fabric choice and yours will too.

Tracing or Pattern Paper

I buy tracing paper by the roll from art supply stores instead of using pattern paper. I use an 18" wide roll for patterns.

> Pro tip: If you have space for it, it is really nice to put your paper in a tabletop gift wrap or butcher wrap dispenser.

Pencil & Eraser

I like to use a mechanical pencil for its precision and erasability. For an eraser, I use a gray kneadable artist eraser since it rubs off the pencil markings only, leaving no paper or eraser dust. You can also mold the eraser into whatever shape you need to get into small areas.

PRESSING

Iron

While it is not used extensively, you do need to press a bra during the construction process. Keep in mind that synthetic fabrics can be damaged, even melted, by excessive heat so always test heat and steam settings on scraps of your fabric before the iron goes near your project. Any basic iron will work. It just needs to have adjustable heat and steam settings.

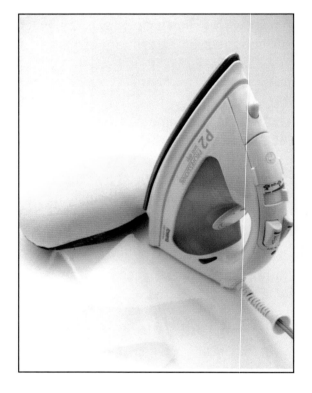

> Pro tip: You must take care not to flatten lace when pressing. A good way to press lace is to put a bath towel under the lace and press from the wrong side using a press cloth.

Press cloth

As with most pressing you should use a press cloth between the iron and your fabric. I generally use a light colored silk organza press cloth since it not only protects the fabric, but also is transparent.

Tailor's Ham

Whenever you press curves, you need a ham. Bra cups have curves so you need a ham for pressing. I recommend a flat bottom ham or using a stand for the traditional tailor's ham to keep both hands free for pressing.

OTHER SUPPLIES

Fray Check

Fray Check is used to seal the underwire casing after it has been stitched closed. Be sure to wipe the top of the bottle and cap it tightly after each use.

Stabilizer

Stabilizer is called for in multiple parts of the bra construction process. You will need to select the best stabilizer for your fabric. I most frequently use strips of nylon sheer — similar to the material that is used for Seams Great. I cut the sheer on the bias or in the direction of the least stretch or give, depending on the fabric.

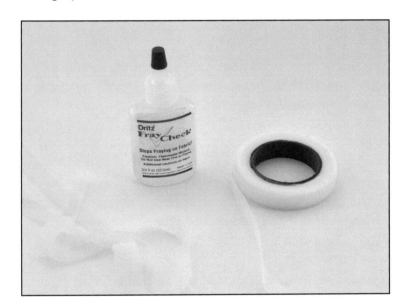

UNDERWIRE HANDLING

Wire Cutter

If you want to trim underwires to custom lengths, you will need a wire cutter. If you plan to cut wires, you also need to add eye protection to your supplies list. You never know where those wire bits are going to fly off to and you don't want it to be into your eye. There is a variety of clear plastic protective eyewear at the hardware store, so please purchase some along with the wire cutter.

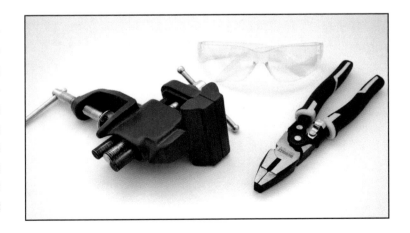

Table Vise

A small table vise that attaches to your worktable holds underwires firmly in place when you are cutting them. It allows you to have both hands free which is safer than trying to hold the wire and cut it at the same time.

Wire Sealer

You will need to seal the cut edges of the underwire so they do not poke through the underwire casing. Household Goop is a cheap and easily available alternative. I discuss how to use Goop in the Cutting Underwires Down to Size section.

DYEING EQUIPMENT

If you plan to dye your fabrics and findings, I recommend using a non-reactive pot that is large enough to hold a ½ yard of 60" wide fabric. Your dye pot should only be used for dyeing.

In terms of the dye itself, I prefer liquid pigment since powdered dye can be tricky to dissolve evenly. Other equipment you will find useful includes a large tea ball strainer and wooden tongs (or similar non-reactive instrument) for extracting small objects from the dye pot. For more information on dyeing, see the section titled "A Short Lesson on Dyeing".

FABRIC MANIPULATION

Spray Adhesive

This is a must if you want to layer fabrics (e.g. put stretch lace over a firmer fabric). Look for one that dissolves on its own after a few days and always test on a scrap of the fabric you will be working with. I explain how to layer fabrics in the Techniques section.

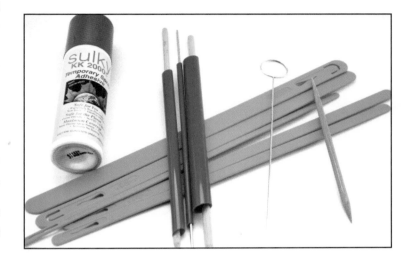

Stiletto

I frequently use a stiletto tool to help me handle small pieces of the bra around the presser foot of the sewing machine. You can find a variety of these tools in the quilting section of the craft store.

Loop Pressing Bars

Intended for 3D appliqué, these come in a pack of five different widths. I use these to press out really nice looking fabric bra straps.

Loop Turner

This tool is useful when making fabric straps. It allows you to quickly turn the fabric to have the right side facing out.

EVALUATING BRA FINDINGS AND NOTIONS

Obtaining bra making notions is no longer the challenge it used to be. You can find a helpful list of sources at http://www.orange-lingerie.com/resources to assist you in your search.

Now that you know where to find them, how do you figure out which ones to buy? In this section, I will review how to determine which findings to purchase to make your bra.

Pro tip: If you cannot find a color match for your project, get white findings and notions and dye them to match. Except for the rings and sliders, bra findings take dye quite well.

RINGS AND SLIDERS

The highest quality and most durable rings and sliders are made of metal. Like many bra findings, the colors are usually limited to white, beige and black and I have never been happy with the durability any of my attempts to change their color. If you can't find a color match to your project, do what I do: use gold or silver rings and sliders or just go with a sturdy clear plastic set.

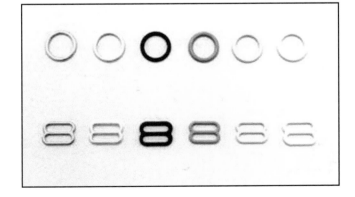

In terms of which size rings and sliders to purchase, you want to match the width of the rings and sliders to the width of the straps so the straps stay put. Your pattern should indicate the size of rings and sliders for its strap design. Where there is no guidance, refer to the Pattern Considerations section of this book to choose the best strap width for your cup size.

UNDERWIRES

Underwires are most commonly made of metal (usually steel) or plastic and come in a variety of diameters and lengths and may be coated in nylon.

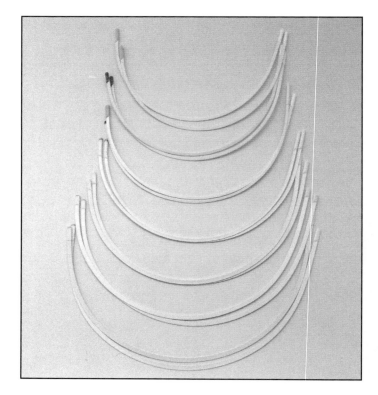

When you have a choice of thinner wires versus thicker wires (I have yet to see a standardized gauge for underwires), use thicker wires for C cups and greater and thinner wires for B cups and smaller. A thinner wire makes it easier to get some of the necessary wire splay for smaller cup sizes. I don't ever recommend plastic underwires since they splay too much across all cup sizes, negatively impacting their ability to provide support.

I address what underwire size to buy in the Testing Underwire Fit section.

You may find that the underwires in your ready-to-wear bra are shaped differently than the underwires you purchase to make your bra. Different brands of bras have different underwire shapes. To some extent you can shape your underwires to resemble the underwires in your favorite bra. I address how to bend wires in the Bending Underwires section.

HOOK AND EYE CLOSURE

My only criterion for the bra closure is that the backing of the eyes be soft, since it will be up against the body. Finished closures are anywhere from 1 hook high to 5 hooks high by 3 hooks long. Because I make a lot of bras with varying closure heights, I find the most versatile and economical solution is to buy hook and eye tape and cut the tape to the height needed for the bra. If you go this route, you will need to seal up the closure along the cut edges once the closure is attached to the bra. I cover this procedure in the Hook and Eyes Closure section.

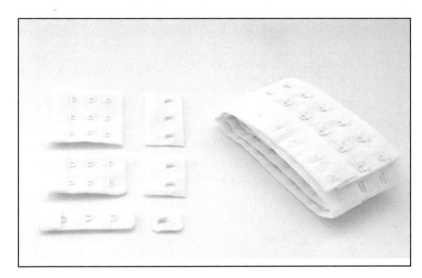

ELASTICS FOR THE UNDERARM AND BAND

High quality elastic is firm with good stretch and good recovery. Lingerie elastic is no exception. The difference with lingerie elastic is that the body facing side has a soft plush finish for comfort. It also usually has a decorative "picot" edge on one side and a flat finish on the opposite edge. Your pattern will dictate the width for elastic.

STRAP ELASTIC

Strap elastic is typically shiny on one side and plush on the body facing side. Your choice of strap elastic should not have any rough or sharp edges.

There should be some stretch to the strap elastic but it should be a firm stretch, 50% tops. I don't recommend using strap elastic for the entire strap, since with its stretch it does not hold the bra firmly in a stable horizontal position on the body. You just need some stretch in the rear of the straps to accommodate body movement.

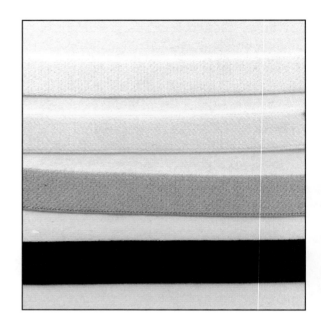

UPPER CUP TRIM

There are many options for finishing the upper cup. You can use the same elastic you use for the underarm area, elastics with fancy trims, or fold over elastic. I prefer to use something with some stretch to it for fitting and wearing ease at the top of the bra cups.

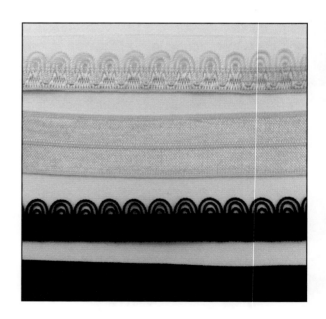

UNDERWIRE CASING, ALSO CALLED UNDERWIRE CHANNELING

I prefer a plush underwire casing since it is soft against the body, as well as strong and durable. Look for a flatter profile plush casing versus a "puffy" one. It is also possible to make your own casing out of a bias cut doubled strip of a lightweight woven fabric.

BOWS/CENTER EMBELLISHMENT (OPTIONAL)

You can attach a variety of embellishments to the center front of your bra. The only criteria I have for a center embellishment is that it be relatively flat. I don't want it to show through clothing.

BONING (OPTIONAL)

Boning is only required if you plan to add support to your band by adding boning to the side seam of the bra. For the most support from side seam boning, use ¼" wide Rigilene boning. Where less support is needed, use ¼" plastic boning, sometimes called Featherlite.

FABRIC

Perhaps more than any other garment, bra patterns are designed for a specific fabric. If you change the fabric, you often radically change the fit of the pattern. Even using a different color of the same fabric can produce a different result since different pigments affect the fabric's properties differently.

Because the results you get from a pattern rely heavily on the fabric choice, I recommend you use the fabric dictated by the pattern you have selected. Ideally the pattern envelope will recommend a fabric and a stretch or give percentage.

Of course, we do not live in an ideal world and I seldom come across a pattern that contains precise information on the fabric properties the pattern was drafted for, leaving much of the decision up to you. So what fabrics should you choose?

Rather than dictate a certain fiber, weave or knit to be used for bra making, I offer fabric selection guidelines. You can apply these guidelines to just about any fabric you encounter to determine if it is suitable for bra making.

THE GUIDING PRINCIPLES OF FABRIC SELECTION

The first thing to know about bra fabric is that its movement is the key to your results. There are two movement concepts; stretch, which means the fabric contains Spandex, and give, which means mechanical movement of the fabric based on its weave or knit. While stretch and give are two different properties, I am going to refer to them jointly as "movement" because that is what we are concerned with when it comes to bra making. If I am only talking about fabrics with Spandex or elastic properties, I will use the term "stretch".

The amount of movement is important since it determines how large the bra cups can expand and determines the overall shape the cup will give the breast. Knowing this, it should come as no surprise that the direction of greatest movement determines the layout of your pattern pieces, not the grain.

The second thing to note about bra fabrics is that you will generally need to use two different fabrics: one for the cups and frame and another for the band.

CUP FABRIC

The fabric for the cups should have little to no movement to contain and provide shape to the breasts. For an everyday supportive bra, I recommend no more than 25% in the direction of greatest movement. This means the other direction has less than 25% movement.

While I like cup fabric to have some movement to allow it to conform to the curves of the body, you can make bra cups out of a fabric with no stretch or give. Just be aware that fitting bras with a rigid fabric is more challenging and you may need to spend more time refining the fit.

> Pro tip: If you want to use a fabric with more movement than your pattern recommends, see the Fabric Manipulation section.

BAND FABRIC

The fabric for the band must have stretch so you can comfortably breathe and move about while wearing the bra. The fabric for the band must balance between the need for movement and the need to provide support while maintaining the correct vertical position on the body. This puts my ideal band fabric at 40% stretch in the direction of greatest movement. Larger cup sizes should use a firm stretch fabric that is closer to 30% stretch for extra support.

> Pro tip: If you cannot find a band fabric to match your cup fabric, you can dye fabric to match. See the section "A Short Lesson on Dyeing".

FRAME AND BRIDGE FABRIC

Because we want the frame and bridge to remain stationary, holding the cups and underwire in the correct position, the fabric for the frame and bridge should have little to no movement horizontally. Any movement in the fabric used for these pieces should be placed vertically. Often the cup fabric is used for the frame and bridge and it is lined with a sheer nylon tricot that has virtually no movement in either direction.

> Pro tip: Examine fabric yardage before it is cut. Knit fabrics can be damaged on the bolt, especially when a bolt is pulled out of the stacks. Some of these fabrics are also prone to snags and pulls. Eye before you buy!

I recommend not making any changes to the fabrics you are using until you have a bra pattern that fits you well. Then you can use your fitted pattern as a base for experimentation. Each time you change the fabric (or the style), it will be a trial and error process to get the proper fit. Just how much of a process depends on how different the fabric is from the original.

> Pro tip: **To quickly fill your lingerie drawer with perfectly fitting bras, find a favorite fabrication and stick to it! When selecting your "go-to" fabric be sure it is either dyeable or comes in a variety of colors for maximum optionality. This will greatly decrease if not eliminate fitting changes and pattern modifications.**

SOMETHING HAS GOT TO GIVE,
OR STRETCH

To determine your fabric's movement properties, you need to determine the direction of greatest movement. Where it is not clear, such as with a 4-way stretch fabric, you will test in both directions (grain and cross grain). If you are using a woven fabric you will want to test the bias.

1. Start by setting a long ruler or tape measure flat on your work surface.

2. Place two pins through a double layer of fabric 5" apart at least 5" from the cut edge and at least 5" away from the selvedge.

3. Grasp the fabric at the pins.

4. While holding the fabric at the 0" mark, pull the fabric with the hand that is at the 5" mark until you feel like it is going to take some physical effort on your part to pull it any more. When fully extended the fabric should still look like it is in a wearable state and it should recover from the test nicely. If it does not, you may have pulled too far.

5. Note the distance the fabric moved. Say for example, the fabric moved to the 8" mark.

6. Calculate the movement percentage by dividing the amount the fabric moved by the total amount of fabric pulled. So if the fabric moved to the 8" mark, or 3" inches (8"-5"), we divide by 5" to get 0.6 or 60% movement.

> Pro tip: Take a measuring tape or ruler with you to the fabric store so you can test fabric movement on the spot.

FABRIC AMOUNTS

Because you must make a trial garment, or toile, out of the fabric you will be using for the final bra, you need to be sure that you have enough fabric to do so. Simply doubling the amount of fabric the pattern recommends is the fastest way to determine your needs the first time you use a new pattern. This will allow plenty of extra fabric for refining the toile as well as for your finished project.

Pro tip: If your fabric choice is expensive, has a decorative edge or a unique pattern, you can always be more precise in determining your fabric needs by laying out the pattern pieces on the fabric itself at the store. Also, if using a rare or expensive fabric, you want to select a fabric with the most similar movement properties as possible for your toile.

MEASURING FOR BRA SIZE

Whenever I talk about bra sizing, I always have to start by saying that there is no size standardization. Each ready-to-wear brand uses different measurements and shapes to come up with their sizing. Pattern makers are no different.

If your pattern maker provides the measurements that their patterns are based on, or the method you should use to measure yourself for their sizing, follow those instructions for determining which size to make. Oftentimes there is no guidance and in those cases you will need to determine which size bra pattern to try.

There are many resources and methods for how to determine your bra size for ready-to-wear and each one has its fans and its detractors. There is no one "correct" method to determine bra size since every body is unique. Following is one method widely used by the big bra manufacturers to determine your band and cup size.

Before you start measuring, forget about your ready-to-wear size. You will be altering your pattern to fit you. You just need to find the best place to start the process.

If you are measuring yourself, be aware that it can be difficult to get an accurate reading since the act of measuring yourself can distort the results. Take each measurement 2 to 3 times to get as accurate a reading as possible.

1. Measure the body's circumference directly under the bust, with the tape measure parallel to floor. To get an accurate measurement, stand up straight, exhale fully and use that reading on the tape as your measurement. Round the measurement to the nearest inch, rounding down if you are at the ½" mark. If your measurement is an even number, add 4" and if it is an odd number, add 5". This is the band size.

Example: If you measure 29", you add 5" to get 34". This means you are a 34 band.

Example: If you measure 38", you add 4" to get 42". This means you are a 42 band.

I will note here that the plus 4 or plus 5 method works best for cup sizes in the A and B cup range and for women with muscular builds. Women with fuller busts may wish to omit the addition and simply use the under bust measurement as their band size. Given the generally vague fabric information from pattern makers and my preference to take fabric in to fit the body, I tend to use the plus 4 or plus 5 to find the band to start with and then alter from there as necessary.

2. Measure around the fullest part of the bust while wearing a bra that is supportive yet out of a relatively thin fabric and preferably not padded. Keeping the tape measure parallel to the floor, stand up straight and exhale fully before you take the reading. Be careful not to pull too tightly.

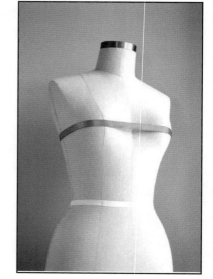

3. Measure the high bust, which is just below the armhole following the same method. You really want your arms to be down at your side, so having a measuring buddy is super helpful.

4. Derive cup size by subtracting the high bust from the full bust. So if we get a full bust measurement of 36" in step 2 and a high bust measurement of 34" in step 3 we get 2" (36" − 34" = 2"). Based on the cup chart below, this is a B cup.

If you are buying a pattern from a company based outside North America, you will need to convert your size into that country's system. Below are two charts to do that: band size and cup size. If you are off the chart or have any sizing questions, you should contact the pattern maker directly, providing your measurements to see what size they recommend for you.

If the difference is:	Your Cup Size is:
0" to ½"	AA
½" to 1"	A
2"	B
3"	C
4"	D
5"	DD or E
6"	DDD or F
7"	G
8"	H
9"	I
10"	J

Cup Size Conversion Chart

USA	UK	France, Spain, Belgium	Italy, Czech	EU, Japan	Australia, New Zealand
AA	AA	AA	--	AA	--
A	A	A	A	A	A
B	B	B	B	B	B
C	C	C	C	C	C
D	D	D	D	D	D
DD or E	DD	E	DD	E	DD
DDD or F	E	F	E	F	E
G	F	G	F	G	F
H	FF	H	FF	H	FF
I	G	J	G	J	G
J	GG	K	GG	K	GG

Band Size Conversion Chart

USA	UK	France, Spain, Belgium	Italy, Czech	EU, Japan	Australia, New Zealand
30	30	80	0	65	8
32	32	85	1	70	10
34	34	90	2	75	12
36	36	95	3	80	14
38	38	100	4	85	16
40	40	105	5	90	18
42	42	110	6	95	20
44	44	115	7	100	22
46	46	120	8	105	24
48	48	125	9	110	26
50	50	130	10	115	28

UNDERWIRE SIZE

To make a bra, you also need to know your underwire size. There are two dimensions to underwire sizes: diameter and length. You are most concerned with the diameter of the underwire since you can easily cut down the length to the exact size you want for your bra pattern. See the Cutting Underwires Down to Size section for instructions on how to do this.

How do you find the right size underwire? The first and easiest place to start is in your lingerie drawer. You can easily open the underwire casing on a bra that fits well and extract the wire. You can always reinsert the wire and close the casing after you test the wire. Even if the wire from your bra does not fit perfectly, you will know where to start.

To determine the wire size, trace it onto transparent paper so you can lay it directly over a supplier's wire chart to easily find the best match. Next, test the wire following the instructions in the following section to insure proper fit.

TESTING UNDERWIRE FIT

An underwire that fits sits directly under the breasts and flat against the body containing the full diameter of the breast tissue without extending into the underarm. At the center front, you want the wire to be at the edge of the breast where it meets the chest wall. To do all this, the underwire must match the diameter of the breasts.

To test the fit of underwires, try them on bare breasts.

1. Lift up the breast and place the wire around the base of the breast where the breast meets the chest wall, the colored tip of the wire at the center front. Align the wire so the bottom of the wire arc is at the base of the breast. If you are doing this alone – tricky but doable – you will need to get in front of a mirror.

2. With the wire in place, raise your arm up and then lower your arm.

3. Judge wire fit.

Signs the wire is too small:

- The wire cannot remain flat on the body

- The wire pokes into the breast

- The wire cannot fit around the breast

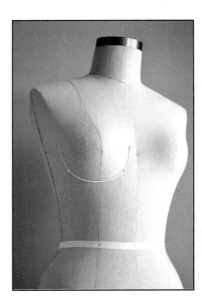

Signs the wire is too large:

- The wire extends past the edge of the breast where it meets the chest wall at the center front

- The wire extends past the breast tissue and into the underarm

- The wire drops below the bottom of the breast onto the chest

Keep in mind that the underwire will splay out a bit toward the underarm once it is in the final bra. This means it is ok if the wire is in contact with breast tissue under the arm.

4. Repeat this process as necessary until you find a wire that fits.

5. Repeat this process for each breast. They may be different!

If the wire you removed from your bra did not pass the fit test, get one to two wire sizes above and below what you traced so you can try on other sizes to get the best fit. If it seems too small, order some larger sizes and if it seems too large, order some smaller sizes. You want a sampling of sizes so you can find the best fit.

Once you have the selection of underwires, run through the test above to find the best fit.

> Pro tip: Before you throw away any worn out bras, harvest the hardware; underwires that still have their shape (if they fit you) and undamaged rings and sliders from the straps can be reused in a new bra.

PATTERN CONSIDERATIONS

Shopping for a bra pattern is in some ways like shopping for other sewing patterns with one major exception - you rarely get to see the finished bra on a model. This complicates things a bit since not everyone uses line drawings to shop for patterns and the character of the pattern illustrations varies widely.

When you look at bra patterns, it's important to look beyond the style of the drawing to the actual seam lines and support features. If you want to create a personal master bra pattern for repeated use and modification, you will want a versatile design that can serve as a solid foundation for all your bra making needs. The following factors should be kept in mind as you shop.

BAND

A and B cups can use either a T back or a scoop back band, both pictured. If you are over a B cup, you want a scooped back band. If you are over a C cup, you will want band scoop band that uses a closure that is more than two hooks and eyes tall. This may be wider than what you are used to, but now that you know a good support-ive bra starts with the band it makes sense.

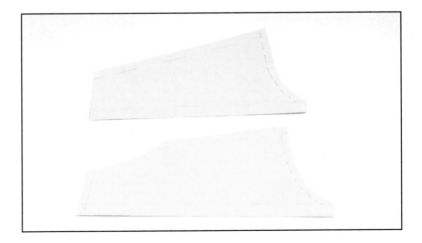

CUPS

Breasts are malleable and will conform to the cup that you put them into so you are looking for an appealing cup shape that will flatter the body. If your breasts are full and round, look for cups with more than two pieces so you have more seams available to shape the cup to accommodate your body. Small cup sizes can select any cup shape they wish.

STRAPS

Straps need to be sufficiently wide to be comfortable and not cut into your skin so you can keep a smooth profile under clothing. My guidelines for strap width are simple: Minimum of ⅜" for B cups and smaller, ¾" straps for C cup up to D cup and 1" wide thereafter.

UNDERWIRES

Love them or hate them - there are benefits to underwire bras. If you decide to eliminate them from your bra, there are four things to know. First, without wires you will not get much support or lift from your bra. Second, not every pattern allows you to simply eliminate the wires. For example, a frameless bra will not work without underwires. Third, if you omit wires from a full frame bra, you still need to apply the underwire casing to strengthen and finish the cup-to-frame seam. Finally, without underwires you may find it difficult to get the bra back to the chest wall at the center front.

PREPPING THE PATTERN

Use your favorite method for prepping and cutting the pattern. Following are some tips to incorporate into your process to produce the most professional looking bra.

1. If necessary, adjust your pattern seam allowances to ¼". This makes it easier to sew tight curves. Careful here – you only want ¼" seam allowances where there is an actual seam. There are areas of the bra that do not have a seam, such as the band where elastic is applied using the edge of the garment as a guideline or a placement line for a scalloped edge of lace.

2. Mark all seam allowances on the pattern. This allows you to walk the seam lines to ensure all the pattern pieces match up nicely. It is also important to have the seam lines marked when it comes time to make any alterations.

3. Check to see the pattern matches the size of your preferred bra findings. If not, you will need to adjust the pattern.

- The band under the cup needs to allow enough room for your band elastic to be turned inward and for the wire casing to be attached and turned as well. This means the area should be at minimum the width of your band elastic plus the ¼" seam allowance for the cup attachment plus ⅛" for an easy turn of the casing and the elastic. If your band elastic is ½" you need a minimum of ⅞" (½" + ¼" + ⅛") space on the frame at the base of the cup.

- The back closure height needs to match up with the height of the hook and eyes you plan to use.

- The width of the underarm elastic and neckline elastic or trim should match the pattern to avoid changing the style lines. If your elastic or trim differs you will need to adjust the pattern to allow for this.

- The strap width should match the size of your rings and sliders for secure straps that stay in place.

- Your underwire needs to fit, or possibly be longer for the pattern, since it can easily be shortened.

4. If you have any pieces that need to be placed on the fold, I recommend creating a full size pattern piece. It is more accurate to cut an entire piece than to place a pattern piece on the fold. This way, your fabric cannot shift and you can better assess any motif or lace placement.

5. To track your pattern changes over time, I recommend tracing the pattern from your source and marking it with the date and sizing information. Each time you make an adjustment, trace a new piece and make the changes from that new piece, marking it with the version number, date and sizing information. Using different color pencils to mark each version makes it even easier to tell the pieces apart.

6. Mark the top and bottom of each pattern piece. It is often difficult to determine the top and bottom of the pattern pieces just from their shape.

7. Be sure to mark the direction of greatest movement on each piece. The direction of movement is placed differently on different pieces and you want to be clear on the correct direction when laying out your pattern on the fabric.

> Pro tip: Once you have perfected your pattern, I urge you to commit the pattern to oak tag or another light card stock. Once you have an oak tag version of the pattern, you can trace the pattern pieces onto the fabric and then cut away the tracing marks. This ensures you will get consistently repeatable results from bra to bra. See the "Replicating Your Success" section for more information.

PATTERN LAYOUT

Lay out the pattern pieces on the fabric as prescribed by your pattern. Because the direction of greatest movement is an important determinant of the layout and it is not as obvious as the grain, mark the direction of greatest movement at the edge of your fabric so you always know where it lies as you arrange the pattern pieces on the fabric. For a refresher on how to determine the direction of greatest movement, see the "Something Has Got to Give or Stretch" section of this book.

> Pro tip: Don't cut multiple bras out simultaneously unless you know for sure that the pattern fits and flatters your figure when made out of the fabric you are cutting. You want to give yourself a chance to make adjustments from one bra to the next.

Mark the following points on your cut pattern pieces. These marks will not just aid in construction but will help you achieve symmetry as you sew your bra:

• Any cup seam match points

• Where the bridge joins to cups, top and bottom

• Where the side frame or band joins to the cup (frameless bra only)

• Where the cup seam meets the bridge, frame or band

- Elastic turn points under the base of the cups (full frame bra only)

- Elastic or trim turn points at underarm, upper cup and center front

Pro tip: Keep in mind that when you are working with a print or lace that motif placement matters. I avoid placing the dominant part of a print over the apex of the breast so I do not get an "X marks the spot". For decorative borders, think about creating a mirrored or balanced look on each side of the bra.

TESTING AND THE TOILE

Unlike other garments, you cannot fit a bra as you sew it. To test the fit, given the close fit and limited to negative ease, you need to make a toile out of the actual fabric you plan to use for your bra. If you decide to use a different fabric for your toile, you can end up with a bra that does not fit as you planned. If your fabric is especially precious, find the closest match possible for your toile to minimize this risk.

There is one key test and pattern change you should do now to make it easier to fit the toile: the bridge test.

THE BRIDGE TEST

This test alone will take you a long way toward getting a great fit from the bra pattern by customizing the spacing between the cups and their corresponding underwires. I always customize the bridge. Always.

To test the bridge of the pattern you will need to make a bridge tester out of oak tag or other light card stock and try it on the body to find the bridge that matches your body.

Following is the process for a full frame bra. For a frameless bra, the bridge tester will be the actual bridge pattern piece, so you can proceed directly to step 4 below.

1. If it is not marked on your pattern, start by drawing a vertical line through the center point of the bridge on the pattern.

2. If the bridge is not a distinct pattern piece, but rather part of the frame, mark a point about midway underneath where the lower cup will be attached to define the end point of the bridge for testing purposes.

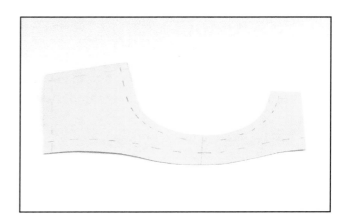

3. Mark the seam lines on the bridge pattern if you have not already done so. You will need these for both the bridge tester and for any alterations as a result of the bridge test.

4. Don't forget that at the top of the bridge there may not be an actual seam line, but an allowance for your trim. You need to mark where the top of the bridge will be after the trim is applied or the seam sewn. For example, if you are applying ⅜" lingerie elastic trim, you need to mark ⅜" down from the top of the pattern piece since you will be folding over that amount of fabric when you turn your trim. Your trim width will vary based on your pattern.

5. Trace the seam lines of the bridge from your pattern for a full frame bra, and along the pattern cutting lines for a frameless bra. Add approximately ¼" to the center for something to hold onto as you manipulate the bridges on the body.

6. Transfer the bridge tracing onto oak tag or card stock. You will need two of these half bridges for the test. I recommend marking the top and the bottom since these pieces start to look the same after awhile.

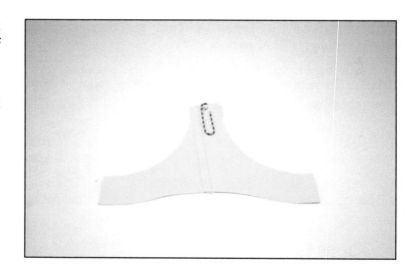

Next, you will try on the bridge by placing the bridge tester pieces between bare breasts to find your breast spacing for the cup and underwire placement for your bra.

Here is how you try on the bridge:

1. Paperclip the two bridge halves together at the center front top.

2. Place the bridge halves against the chest between the between the breasts and pull the bottom of the bridge pieces apart, or push together, until the curved edge of each piece is positioned where the breasts meet the chest wall. Be sure to keep the bridge flat against the chest. Depending on

your cup size, you may need to lift the breasts up to locate this spot. Here is where creative use of mirrors or a fitting friend will be a big help.

If necessary, you can fold the edges of the top of the bridge over if it is too wide for your body. The entire purpose of this exercise is to find the correct breast spacing for your body.

3. Now, the tricky part. You need to remove the bridge pieces from their fitted position on the body without altering the positioning of either half. To do this I recommend moving the bridge down along the body then lifting away.

4. Once removed, lay the bridge tester on a sheet of paper and trace it in its entirety.

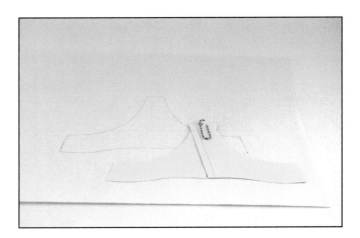

I usually test the bridge two or three times, tracing after each test to be sure I am getting consistent results.

Now you can customize your pattern using the tracing from the bridge test.

1. Draw a line through the center of your tracing. I do this by folding the tracing in half, matching up each side, then drawing a line through the fold.

2. Trace the half bridge from your tester.

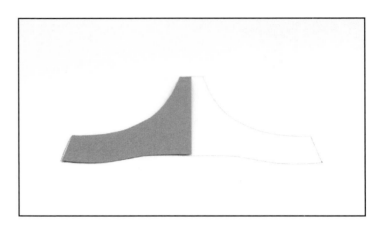

Now to customize the pattern's bridge. This process varies based on whether you are making a full frame or frameless bra. Here is what to do for a full frame bra:

1. Align the top of your customized bridge piece to the trim line point or seam line at the top of your pattern's bridge.

2. Pivot your bridge tester tracing until it aligns with the cup seam line. This will likely alter the width and/or angle of the center front.

3. Mark the new center front line based on your bridge tester.

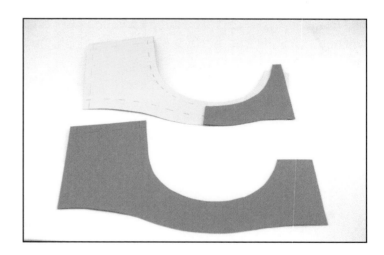

For a frameless bra, your tester bridge is now the bridge for the pattern itself. You just need to add back the room for any trim or seam allowance to the top of the bridge.

Your pattern's bridge is now customized, placing the cups and underwire in the correct location for your body and there should be no fitting issues in that area going forward.

CONSTRUCTING THE TOILE

For the toile construction you can omit attaching the elastics and trims. Your goal is to have a bra that you can put on the body to assess the fit and style lines. Depending on your fabric and the required alterations, you may be able to take your toile apart and reuse it to make your final bra. To make it easier to take the toile apart, use contrasting thread to baste the toile together.

If you have any questions about any of the steps below, refer to the Techniques section of this book.

The assembly order for the toile is as follows:

1. Cut out and mark the bra following the Prepping the Pattern and Pattern Layout instructions

2. Baste cups together

3. Baste a strip of stabilizer to top of each upper cup

4. Baste a strip of stabilizer to the underarm area of each cup

5. Baste frame pieces together (if applicable)

6. Baste frame to band (if applicable)

7. Baste a strip of stabilizer across the top of the bridge

8. Baste the cups to the frame (full frame) or to the bridge and the band (frameless)

9. Baste the underwire casing around each cup

10. Baste "topstitch" underwire casing to the frame (full frame) or bra cups (frameless)

11. Baste straps together based on your bra pattern style

12. Baste the front of the straps to each upper cup at their indicated attachment point

13. Baste the back of the straps to the back of band at their indicated attachment point

14. Baste hook and eye fastener onto band

15. Baste front and back straps together

16. Insert underwires

Be sure your basting is secure at each end of the seam line so it does not come undone when the bra is placed on the body. A bra is under stress on the body and you need a stable garment to make it through the fitting.

Pro tip: If you will be adding decorative stitching to the upper cup, it can change the fit of the area. Test the stitching embellishment in the toile phase to be sure the shrinkage from the stitching embellishment does not affect the fit.

Now you can try on the toile to assess the fit.

FITTING

Because a pattern is only a starting point for your custom garment, you will inevitably need to make some alterations to the toile to get the best fitting bra. While fitting and pattern alterations are topics worthy of an entire book, the following are the most common fitting challenges and their solutions.

Throughout the fitting sections, I am going to make the assumption that you are following your pattern's guidelines when it comes to fabric choices. If you are not, that is the first thing to check. If your fabric has different movement properties than what your pattern is designed for, it will be more of a trial and error process to get the correct fit.

Also, before you start any fitting analysis, I assume that you performed the bridge test and altered your pattern accordingly. You will also want to fit your underwire following the instructions in the Testing Underwire Fit section. Having solved for these factors removes two fitting variables from the equation. Do not proceed until you have completed these two tasks.

Finally, the fitting section is written in the order that you should fit your bra: band and frame, straps and then finally the cups. As I proceed through the fitting section, I assume that any prior issue has been resolved. This means that you cannot just skip to the "cup gapes under the arm" without first examining the other issues in order. Proceeding through the fitting in order will get you to a fitting resolution faster.

As you work through the fitting process, only adjust one variable at a time since one change will often impact other areas. For example, it may look like there is a problem with the cups but once you have the strap at the correct length in the correct position, the cup fits beautifully. So, make one adjustment, retest the fit and so on until the bra fits.

Pro tip: Take pictures as you fit your garment. It helps you look more objectively at the fit and helps document your fitting process over time. Be sure to record the time and date of your picture along with any notes, to assess which alterations produced the pictured result. This will allow you to go back to a prior revision, if so desired.

Just a few more notes before you dive in to fitting! I assume that you have experience altering patterns, and when making pattern changes that you are working with pattern pieces that have no seam allowances. To keep this section streamlined and focused on which changes to make and where to make them, I will not be reminding you to add or subtract elastic or seam allowances.

Also, throughout the illustrations of the pattern changes, I show the original pattern in blue and the altered pattern in orange. Note that a two-piece horizontal seam cup is used throughout the pictures. Your style lines may vary but the concepts remain the same.

BAND AND FRAME

Issue: The band rides up the back. Front of the bra is fine.

Diagnosis: The band is too loose.

Solution: First, be sure the band is actually too large. The band of the toile may feel a bit loose since there are no elastics in the bra. Recall that only two fingers should fit under the band when the bra is done at its loosest row of hooks. Since there is no elastic in the band, take care to not over stretch the band fabric as you test this.

If the band is too big, you need to decrease the length. This change is not made at the back of the band where it would move the back straps closer together.

1. Estimate the total amount the band needs to be decreased.

2. Remove half this amount from each side seam. If your pattern has no side seam, mark the toile at the underarm and slash and overlap the pattern there.

3. Redraw the back band angle and underarm area as necessary, taking care not to change the height of the band at either end.

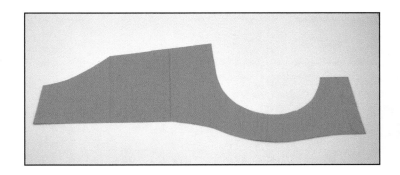

Issue: The bra is cantilevered forward under the weight of the breasts causing the band to ride up the back. The breasts weigh down the bra in the front.

Diagnosis: There are three potential causes:

1. The band is too big (see The Band is Too Loose above)

2. The band fabric is too stretchy or too lightweight to provide support for a larger cup size

3. The band is not ideally structured for your cup size

Solution: The solution depends on the degree to which the bra is pulled down at the front. After you test the band and adjust its length if necessary, there are four alternatives.

1. If the band is the correct size, use a heavier weight and lower stretch fabric for the band. For large cup sizes, I use a maximum stretch of 30% for the band. This often means increasing the length of the band due to the decreased stretch.

2. If the band is the correct size, increase the width of elastic used in the band at both the top and bottom of the band. At the bottom of the band, add the additional width as required for the elastic. Do the same at the bottom of the frame and bridge. See "The underarm area is too low" diagnosis in this section for how to add room at the top of the band and the neighboring pattern pieces.

3. If the band is the correct size, increase the width of the band to increase the support of the bra. The methods to increasing the band, in order of preference: add a scoop back (if none is present), increase the hook and eye closure height or raise the underarm. Each approach is described in this section.

4. If the band is the correct size, add boning to the side seam of the bra. See the Side Boning section for details on how to do this.

Add a scoop back:

1. Draw a vertical line from the point where the back straps attach to the bra.

2. Draw a 20-degree downward sloping line from the wire line of the bra (the cup to frame seam line) toward to the line you made in step 1 above. If your bra has a side seam, you will first need to place the frame and band pieces together at the side seam before drawing this line.

3. Draw a gently curving scoop from the top of the hook and eye closure to the point where the lines from step 1 and step 2 intersect.

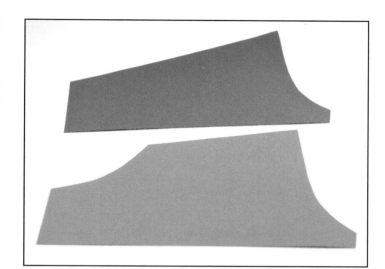

Increase hook and eye closure height:

1. Measure the height of the new, taller hook and eye closure.

2. Add to the existing closure height to match the height of the taller closure.

3. Redraw the back scoop or the angle of the T back as necessary.

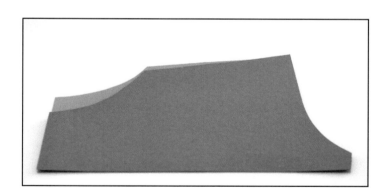

Issue: Breathing is uncomfortable. The bra is digging in to the body.

Diagnosis: The band is too tight or the cups are too small.

Solution: The first thing to address is the band unless the cups are clearly too small, meaning the breasts are coming out from underneath and over the top of the cups. If that is the case, try a larger cup size then begin the fitting process.

1. Check your fabric. Is the stretch aligned so it goes around the body? If not, recut the band so the stretch is correctly oriented and retest.

2. If the stretch is correct and the band is too small, increase the length. This change is not made at the back of the band where it would move the straps farther apart.

a. Estimate the total amount the band needs to be increased.

b. Add half this amount to each side seam. If your pattern has no side seam, mark the toile at the underarm and slash and spread the pattern there.

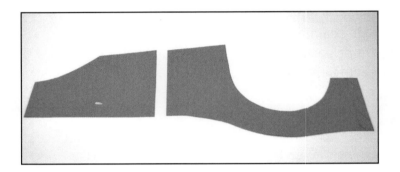

c. Redraw the back band angle and underarm area as necessary, taking care not to change the height of the band at either end.

Issue: The bra feels like it is in the armpit. It feels like the bra is cutting into the area under the arm. The bra irritates the underarm.

Diagnosis: The underarm area is too high.

Solution: Lower the height of the bra at the underarm.

1. This change affects the cups, frame and band. Lay out these pattern pieces on top of another sheet of paper, matching them up at their seam lines at the underarm.

2. Tape the joined pattern pieces to the paper.

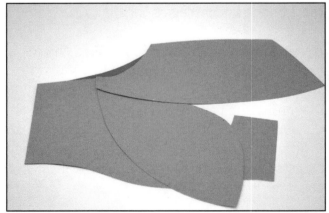

3. Draw in the new desired underarm height and cut the revised pattern pieces from the paper.

Note lowering the underarm may force you to use a shorter underwire.

Issue: The bra does not feel like it is covering the area under the arm. The body feels overexposed on the sides of the bra.

Diagnosis: The underarm area is too low.

Solution: Raise the height of the bra at the underarm.

1. This change affects the cups, frame and band. Lay these pattern pieces on top of a separate sheet of paper, matching them up at their seam lines at the underarm.

2. Tape the joined pattern pieces to the paper.

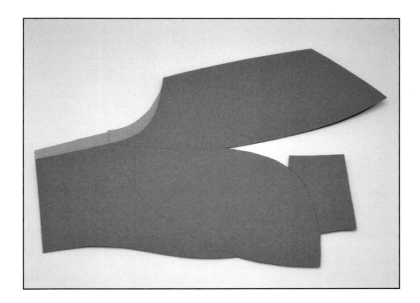

3. Draw in the new desired underarm height and cut the revised pattern pieces from the paper.

Note: Raising the height of the underarm may force you to use a longer wire.

STRAPS

Issue: The straps dig into the shoulders. You cannot get the straps over the shoulders to get the bra placed properly on the body.

Diagnosis: The straps are too tight.

Solution: If you have a two-piece strap, a front portion with no movement and back elasticized portion, determine first where to add the length. If the straps are too short to get the bra on your body, you may need to hang the bra over one shoulder to estimate the amount and where to add.

1. If the front strap could go all the way over the shoulder, then the front strap length is fine. If it is too short to do so, add to the front strap so it can reach entirely over the shoulder. To maintain the size of the strap at each end, add the desired amount to the strap in the center and then redraw any style lines.

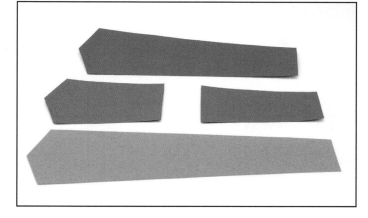

2. If the front strap length is fine per the above, then add to the back strap by cutting a longer length of elastic. Do the same if you have a one-piece strap.

Be sure to add enough additional length to allow you to adjust the strap. You do not want the ring and slider jammed together with the bra strap extended to its maximum length since this would wear out any elastic rather quickly.

Issue: Bra straps are falling off the shoulder. Straps hang loosely over the shoulders.

Diagnosis: The straps are too loose or the straps are positioned too far out on the shoulder.

Solution: First focus on the length of the straps. Strap placement is covered next in this section.

Start by determining the amount to decrease the straps by pinching out the excess at the shoulder. If you have a two-piece strap, a front portion with no movement and back elasticized portion, you need to determine where to decrease the length next.

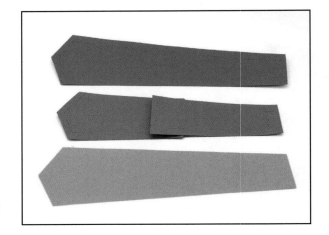

1. If the front strap extends down the back, it should be decreased. Shorten it so that it only goes all the way around the shoulder. To maintain the size of the strap at each end, subtract the desired amount to the strap in the center and then redraw any style lines.

2. If the front of the strap is the correct length, decrease the length of the back strap elastic by cutting it shorter. Do the same if you have a one-piece strap.

Issue: Looking at the front of the bra, the bra straps are not sitting at the mid point of the shoulder. The straps are closer to the neck, perhaps uncomfortably close.

Diagnosis: The straps are placed too far toward the neck. You should also check the back strap placement as described in this section.

Solution: Move the straps out to your desired location.

To move straps outward, first determine the distance you need to move the straps out to get them into the correct position. Next, slice across the top of the upper cup of your pattern and slide the cut piece out toward the shoulder. Then, redraw the style lines of the upper cup.

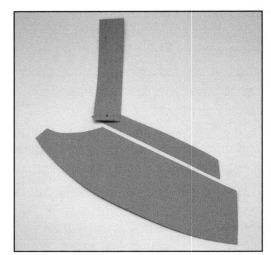

Issue: Looking at the front of the bra, the bra straps are closer to the edge of the shoulder or even off the shoulder.

Diagnosis: The straps are placed too far toward the shoulder. You should also check the back strap placement as described in this section.

Solution: Move the straps to your desired location.

To move straps inward, first estimate the distance you need to move the straps in to get them into the correct position. Next, slice across the top of the upper cup of your pattern and slide the cut piece in toward the center front. Then, redraw the style lines of the upper cup.

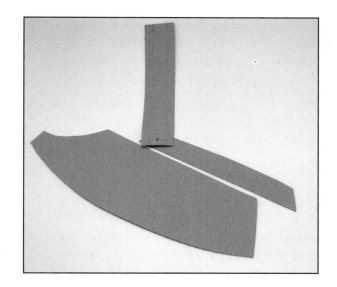

Issue: Looking at the back of the bra, the straps are too close the arms, the straps feel too far out on the back or the straps are falling off the shoulder.

Diagnosis: Back straps are too far out toward shoulder.

Solution: Move the straps in to your desired location. After you determine the distance you want to move the straps, redraw the back scoop so it ends at the desired strap placement point at the top of the band. For a T-back bra, you can simply move the straps over to where you want them.

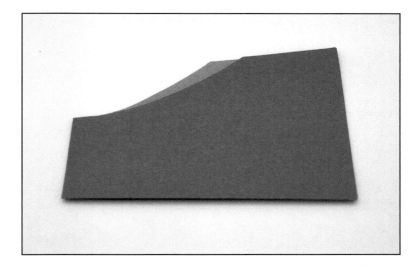

Issue: Looking at the back of the bra, the straps are too close to the center of the back or the straps feel too close to the neck.

Diagnosis: Back straps are too far in toward the center.

Solution: Move the straps out to your desired location. After you determine the distance you want to move the straps, redraw the back scoop so it ends at the desired strap placement point at the top of the band. Draw in

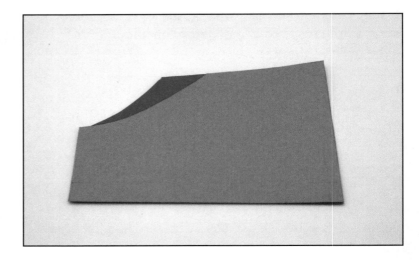

any necessary addition to the top of the back band, following the angle of the existing line. For a T-back bra, you can simply move the straps over to where you want them.

CUPS

Before you fit the cups, you must have completed all the prior steps: fitting your underwire, customizing your bridge and fitting the band and the straps. If you have any cup fitting issues after completing those steps, proceed through this section.

Issue: There are folds or wrinkles in the cups. There is some excess fabric in the cups.

Diagnosis: The cups are too large.

Solution: If you can pinch more than ½" excess fabric across the cups, move to a smaller cup size.

If the excess fabric is less than ½", decrease the cup volume by reducing the arc at the fullest part of the cup seam line. Leave the parts of the cup that join to the frame and wire line unchanged.

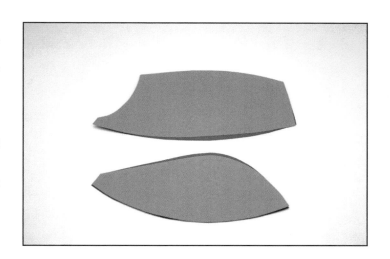

Issue: The cups gapes at the underarm, and otherwise the cups fit well.

Diagnosis: The breast shape does not require an allowance for volume in the underarm area.

Solution: Remove the excess fabric from the cups at the underarm.

1. Pin out the excess fabric from the cup like you are taking a dart.

2. Measure the amount of the dart at the underarm and the distance from the underarm to the end point of the dart.

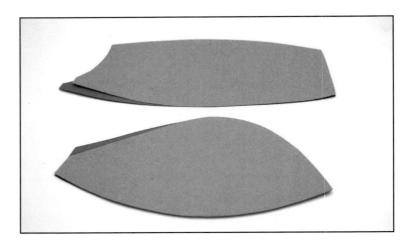

3. Remove the amount of the dart from the cup, tapering the decrease to zero at the end point of the pinned dart.

4. Smooth and redraw the lines on the pattern piece.

Do not try to fix this issue via the underarm elastic. You do not want rippled bra cups and you do not want to shorten the life of the bra by forcing the elastic to stretch to its maximum with each wearing.

Issue: The cups are stretched tight across the breasts, the breasts feel pinched in the cups, the cups do not cover the breasts, the breasts come out from underneath the cups, or the body bulges over and around the cups of the bra.

Diagnosis: The cups are too small.

Solution: When the cups of the bra are too small, my preference is to directly move to a larger cup size since I find it easier to take in and tailor versus experiment with adding additional volume. If the breasts are covered and contained but there remains an overall tightness in the cups, you can experiment adding volume to the cups by increasing at the fullest part of the cup seam line. Leave the parts of the cup that join to the frame and wire line unchanged.

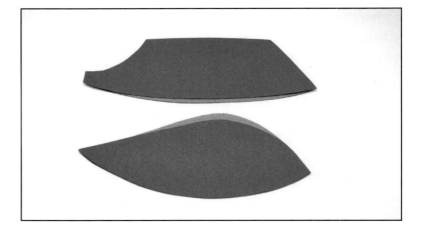

Note: if the larger cups do not fit nicely into the existing frame, adjust for this by decreasing the cups at the underarm. This is illustrated in the next fitting issue below.

Issue: The center front of the bra does not come back to the chest wall.

Diagnosis: Cups are too small.

Solution: Try the next larger cup size without changing the frame or band. If the larger cups do not fit nicely into the frame, adjust for this by decreasing the cups at the underarm.

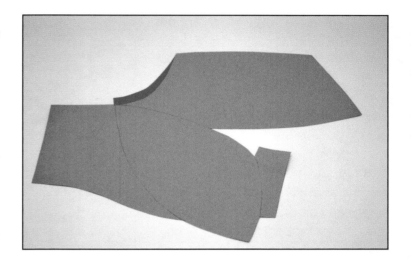

Issue: The cups looks great everywhere, but there is a bit of excess fabric at the base of the breast in the lower cups. If there is a lot of excess fabric wrinkled at the bottom of the cups, skip to the next topic in this section.

Diagnosis: The breast has more flatness at the base than the cup shape.

Solution: Flatten the curve at the lower edge of the lower cups. Start small with a ⅛" decrease, and if the issue remains unresolved try an additional ⅛". If the flat area still remains after ¼" worth of decreases, skip to the next topic in this section. The cup is either too small or not providing enough roundness for the breast shape.

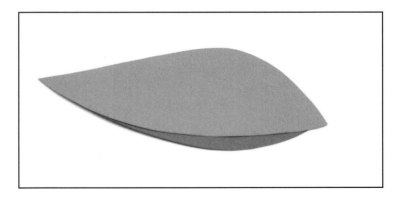

Issue: The cups look great but there is a fair amount of fabric wrinkled at the bottom of the cups.

Diagnosis: The breasts cannot drop all the way into the cups. The cups are either too small or they do not accommodate a rounder breast shape.

Solution: Before you make any pattern alterations, try a larger cup size.

If a larger cup size did not work, change your pattern to a three-piece cup. A three-piece cup is good for rounder breasts since it provides more seam lines that can be used for shaping.

1. To convert a two-piece cup to a three-piece cup, slice the bottom cup vertically along a line that starts at the top at the fullest point of the cup and extends down to the bottom of the cup.

2. Mark the midpoint of each piece along the cut line.

3. Mark out from the midpoint, in step 2 above, from ⅛" to ⅜" such that you can draw an arc. The distance to place this mark depends on the amount of roundness you need to create in the cup.

4. Draw an arc using the midpoint mark from step 3 as the apex of the arc, taking care not to change the top or bottom seam lines of the cup.

If you already have a three-piece cup, increase the arc of the seam joining the cup pieces.

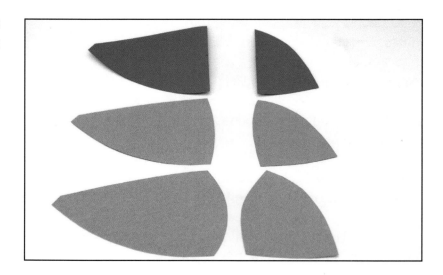

Issue: There is an appearance of "quadra-boob" as the upper cups press into the body tissue. The fit of the lower cup is good.

Diagnosis: The upper cup is too tight.

Solution: Add length to the upper cups. First estimate the additional length necessary, then slash and spread the pattern accordingly at about the mid point of the upper cup

pattern piece. Redraw the style lines of the upper cup. Note: the upper cup remains unchanged at the wire line even though the angle of the seam line has changed.

Issue: The upper cups do not lie flat against the body. There is extra room in the upper cup. The fit of the lower cup is good.

Diagnosis: The upper cups are too loose.

Solution: Decrease the length of the upper cups by pinching out a dart from the center of the upper cup.

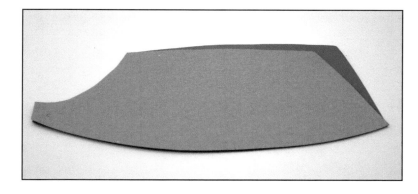

Next, slash and overlap the upper cup pattern by this amount at about the midpoint of the upper cup pattern piece. Redraw the style lines. Retest. Note: the upper cup remains unchanged at the wire line even though the angle of the seam line has changed.

TECHNIQUES

In the following sections I explain the techniques used to make a bra. For those techniques most regularly left unexplained by books and patterns, I go into the most detail. For more frequently explored techniques, I provide helpful tips to help you get professional looking results.

Before you start sewing your bra together, you will need to test your machine's stitch and tension settings, your tools, etc. on scraps of the fabric you are using. It is far better to make any necessary adjustments on scraps rather than on your garment.

Pro tip: If you are new to bra making, consider practicing each of the following techniques on fabric scraps before starting your bra project.

CONSTRUCTION SEQUENCE

The construction sequence for bras varies by pattern. While there are certain areas where it is best to follow the pattern's instructions, such as the order of construction of the cups, you can usually follow my preferred construction sequence. Please read through your pattern's instructions first!

For each step of the construction process, I refer you to the section that contains more detail.

1. Sew cup pieces together, topstitch and trim seam allowances in the order prescribed by your pattern. The order of operations makes a difference in cup construction.

See Sewing Seams and Topstitching for instructions.

2. Finish the upper cup via your preferred or pattern-directed method. Take care to follow any of your pattern's instructions regarding straps at this stage. Straps may be directly attached to the upper cup, which is different from my favorite attachment. This would mean creating any straps prior to finishing the upper cup.

To finish the upper cups, see Attaching Lingerie Elastic and The Finished Upper Cup sections.

3. Finish the bridge via your preferred or pattern-directed method.

See Clean Finished Bridge section for one method.

4. Sew frame together if it is in multiple pieces and topstitch seams.

5. If your bra has a side seam, sew the band to the frame and topstitch the seam to the frame side of the bra. If you plan to add side boning, omit the topstitching and attach the boning casing to the seam allowance. See the Side Boning section for details.

6. If you are making a frameless bra, attach band elastic to the bottom of the band. This must be done before you attach it to the cups. If you have a T back bra and want to enclose the back strap under the band elastic, do that as part of the second pass of sewing on the elastic. This means creating your back straps prior to this step. See the Attaching Lingerie Elastic and Straps sections for details.

7. Sew the cups to the bra. If making a full frame bra, the cups are sewn into the frame. If making a frameless bra, the cups are attached to the side or band and the bridge. I do this in one continuous seam so the bottoms of the cups are marked with ¼" stitching for aligning the underwire casing attachment.

8. If making a full frame bra, attach the band elastic after sewing in the cups but before attaching the casing. If you have a T back bra and want to enclose the back strap under the band elastic, do that as part of the second pass of sewing on the elastic. This means creating your back straps prior to this step. See the Attaching Lingerie Elastic and Straps sections for details.

9. Attach underwire casing to the cup seam line and topstitch to secure in place. Do not insert the wires or seal the casing at the center front yet.

Note: attaching the underwire casing includes attaching the underarm elastic and, if you are using a ring to attach the front straps, that is also included in this step. See the Attaching Lingerie Elastic and Attaching Underwire Casing sections for details.

10. Create back straps.

Instructions can be found in the Straps section.

11. Attach back straps if you have a scoop back bra. If you have a T back bra, secure the straps to the upper edge of the band at the elastic.

See the Straps section for details.

12. Attach hook and eye closure.

See Hook and Eye Closure section for details on this procedure.

13. Attach front straps through the upper cup rings if you have not already attached straps to the upper cup. See Front Straps section for instructions.

14. If you are using side boning, now is the time to insert the boning, topstitch and seal up the casing. See the Side Boning section for details.

15. Insert underwires and seal wire casing at the center front.

See the final step of Attaching Underwire Casing for instructions.

16. Attach front straps to the back straps by threading the front strap though the ring attached to the back loop and sewing a bar tack or two straight rows of stitching to secure.

17. Attach bow or other center front embellishment as desired.

See Attaching Bow/Centerpiece Decoration section for additional information.

18. Inspect your handiwork, trim any loose threads, then try on your new bra!

SEWING SEAMS

For the seams of the bra, use a straight stitch set at a 2.5mm length to get nice clean lines. You may be surprised to be using a straight stitch on fabrics that have movement. However, unless the fabric is very stretchy, a straight stitch will give you beautiful and durable seams. If your fabric is very stretchy, use the "lightning stitch" which is a very small zigzag stitch for seams.

As discussed the Prepping the Pattern section, all seam allowances should be at ¼". I like to use my machine's ¼" setting, which positions the needle for ¼" seam when the fabric edge is lined up with the edge of the presser foot. If the fabric is particularly problematic, I will go to the trouble of using a straight stitch throat plate and a ¼" foot.

> Pro tip: Write down the stitch and tension settings for each fabric you use as well as for each part of the construction process. Depending on how you achieve your ¼" seams, you may want to record your method for future reference.

You may wonder why I don't recommend marking and sewing along the seam lines since bras call for precision sewing. There are a couple of reasons I do not take this approach for bras. First, there are few actual seam lines; many fabric edges are just elastic guides. Second, bra fabrics can be problematic in terms of the visibility and subsequent removal of markings. I don't want to take the risk. Not marking the seam lines means careful sewing throughout. Of course, if marking the seam lines works better for you, go for it.

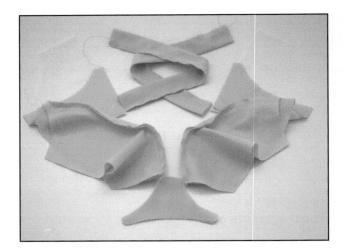

Pro tip: I like to sew as many pieces together as possible, without stopping, before I have to get up to press or change machine settings. If the same color of thread can be used throughout, I sew the cups, bridge, band and straps together in one continuous seam.

TOPSTITCHING

Keep the fabric taut on either side of the seam as you topstitch. You want to be sure the seam is fully open, especially since the bra will be under stress when worn. Just don't pull the fabric from front to back. This makes for a wavy seam finish.

I vary my topstitching based on the fabric and the look I am going for. Sometimes I want the look of a zigzag over the cross-cup seam or I may want to stitch as far away from the seam line as possible. You can position the topstitching according to your preferences, just so long as the seam allowance is caught under the topstitching and there are no puckers or folds in the fabric.

Following are a couple of notes on correcting stitching. First, you can only rip out stitching so many times before the fabric is weakened or even ruined. The number of times depends on your fabric, but you will definitely know when you have gone too far. Second, no one but you will examine the bra's topstitching from under your microscope. The only reason to tear out topstitching is if: (a) there is an obvious fold or pucker in the fabric, (b) there is loose seam allowance on the wrong side of the fabric or (c) it looks bad from 3 feet away. If any of those circumstances apply, then go ahead and make the correction, but do so carefully.

When removing stitching, be certain you know what you are ripping into. Some fabrics have open work and fine threads that could easily be mistaken for your sewing thread. Some bra fabrics are also prone to snagging. Be sure you are ripping the sewing thread and not the fabric.

> Pro tip: Use thread colors purposefully. You can make a bra beautiful inside and out by matching thread to both the wrong and right sides of the fabric or you can create a striking contrast to change the overall look of the bra.

TRIMMING SEAM ALLOWANCES

Depending on the positioning of your topstitching, it may be necessary to trim excess seam allowance to eliminate bulk.

To do this, start by cutting the seam allowance that is farthest away from you as you hold the piece using offset or duck billed scissors (see Equipment and Supplies for details). Gently pull the far side of the cup down by wrapping it around the hand holding the cup. This helps to isolate the seam allowance to allow for easier identification and cutting.

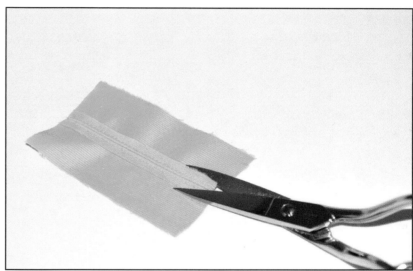

THE FINISHED UPPER CUP

I recommend attaching any upper cup trim to the completed cup after sewing, and topstitching the cup seams rather than waiting until the cups are attached to the rest of the bra. I always get a better result that way, since it eliminates the need to negotiate the abrupt corner from the cup to the bridge. If you follow this approach you must also pre-finish the top of the bridge (see The Clean Finished Bridge section) before sewing it to the cups. This may deviate from your pattern's instructions.

Exact upper cup trim depends on the style of bra you are making. As discussed in the Supplies section, you can use a variety of trims and elastics to finish this area. I like to use a finish with some stretch, so the most common finish I use is detailed in the Attaching Lingerie Elastic section. However, when using lace, I want the scalloped edge of the lace to be visible and I want the upper cup stabilized so it does not stretch out of shape.

For a lace upper cup, there are two approaches and the approach varies by type of lace. For a stretch lace, I zigzag clear elastic or a narrow color-matched elastic called décolleté elastic on the inside of the bra underneath the scallops. For rigid lace, I apply a small strip of stabilizer on the inside of the bra underneath the scallops. Both treatments are applied before the cups are sewn to the rest of the bra to capture the ends of each treatment in subsequent construction steps.

Stabilizing a stretch lace upper cup:

1. Measure and cut elastic.

Lay ¼" clear un-stretched elastic across the entire upper cup to measure the length needed. If your elastic is wider than ¼," you will have to trim it down to match your stitching after attaching it.

2. Switch to a Universal needle. This needle does a better job penetrating the clear elastic than the Stretch needle.

3. Attach your Teflon sewing machine foot if you have one. This will help the machine glide more easily over the clear elastic which can be 'sticky'.

4. Set your sewing machine to a 3-step zigzag stitch.

5. With the elastic side up, on the wrong side of the bra, sew the elastic across the entire length of top of the upper cup, aligning it with the lower parts of the lace scallops. Do not stretch the elastic as you sew it.

6. If the elastic was wider than ¼" or is wider than your 3-step zigzag, trim it very carefully using offset scissors. The stitch width should cover the entire width of the clear elastic so it will not turn back on itself when the bra is worn.

Attach décolleté elastic the same way as above but do not trim the width to match your stitching. When attaching décolleté elastic, you will need to adjust the width of your zigzag to just match the width of the elastic. Test this on a swatch of scrap fabric before applying the elastic to the upper cup of your bra.

> Pro tip: While clear elastic can withstand trimming since it is essentially a strip of plastic, other elastics are braided, woven or knitted and their integrity will be damaged with trimming. You do not want to cut the bra's life short by cutting elastics.

Stabilizing a Rigid Lace Upper Cup:

1. Measure and cut stabilizer.

Measure the length of the top of the upper cup. That is the length of stabilizer you will need for each cup.

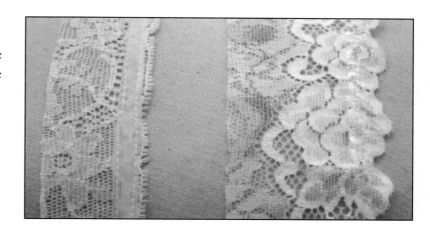

2. Cut a ¾" strip of stabilizer the length of the upper cup, fold in three and press to get a ¼" strip. If your stabilizer material will fray, you will need to create a flat and finished ¼" strip of stabilizer.

3. Using a 2.5mm straight stitch with the stabilizer side up on the wrong side of the bra, sew the strip across the entire length of the top of the upper cup, aligning it with the lower parts of the lace scallops. Repeat the straight stitch at the bottom of the stabilizer to secure.

THE CLEAN FINISHED BRIDGE

Bridge finishes vary with the style of the bra. Regardless of your finishing choice, this area needs to be stabilized with a suitable lightweight low to no movement fabric. Frequently this will be sheer nylon tricot, but it could also be thin lightweight pretreated cotton, silk organza or even the fashion fabric.

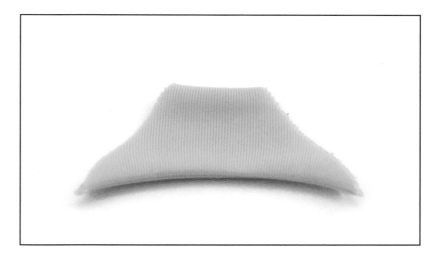

I like using the bridge stabilizer to create a clean finish without the addition of any trim or elastic, to avoid unnecessary bulk in this small area. The key technique to a professional-looking clean finished bridge takes a cue from tailoring by building in "favoring." The first step is to draft a proper facing pattern piece to use for cutting out your stabilizer.

1. Trace your bridge from the pattern along the cutting lines onto a separate sheet of paper. If you are working with a full frame style, the bridge extends on the frame to roughly the midpoint of the lower cup.

2. Mark a line $\frac{1}{16}$" down from the upper edge of the cup. This is the cutting line for the top of the bridge facing.

3. For frameless styles only, mark a line $\frac{1}{16}$" up from the lower edge of the cup. This is the cutting line for the bottom of the bridge facing.

4. Cut out the bridge facing pattern piece from your stabilizer along the cutting lines. Remember: since this is a stabilizing piece, any movement should be oriented in the vertical direction only, just as it is with the bridge.

Once you have your facing piece, to finish the bridge cleanly:

1. Using a straight stitch, sew the facing to the bridge with the right sides of the fabric together.

> Pro tip: Sew from the center to the outside when attaching the bridge facing. It allows for better handling and more accurate seaming on these tiny pieces. Just be sure to trim the interior threads; you do not want any bulk trapped inside the bridge. For basting and for sewing the bridge to the cups, I stitch from the top down to ensure I get a perfect matching of the two pieces at the top of the bra.

2. Press the seam allowance to the stabilizer side of the bridge.

3. Understitch the stabilizer facing to the upper bridge seam allowance near the seam line, then press favoring the right side.

4. For frameless styles only, clean finish the bottom of the bridge as above, necessarily omitting the understitching. After stitching, double-check the bridge for symmetry. If the bridge is not symmetrical, re-stitch or recut and re-sew the bridge, which is often faster. Press the bridge once you have achieved symmetry.

5. For full frame styles, baste the facing just inside the cup seam lines. It will make it easier to sew in the cups.

6. For frameless styles, baste the raw edges of the bridge together at just under ¼". This will help you line up the bridge and still allow for easy removal of the basting.

ATTACHING LINGERIE ELASTIC

Each pattern may vary, but there are four potential places that you will attach lingerie elastic: the upper cup, the underarm, the bridge and the band. Here I will cover the most common lingerie elastic trim treatment used in bra making. The elastic is attached in a two step process, a regular zigzag stitch for the first pass and a 3-step zigzag stitch after the curves have been clipped, the fabric trimmed and the elastic has been turned to the inside of the bra.

1. Measure the elastic.

To get the correct length of elastic, lay it flat along the piece or section that it will to be attached to. I add about ½" on each side of the required length to facilitate handling and allow for turning over outward curves.

2. Select the visible edge of the elastic.

Decide which edge of the lingerie elastic you want to show on the right side of the final bra: the picot (ridged) edge or the flat edge. For the example pictured, the picot edge will be the visible edge of the elastic. The smooth edge of the elastic will be turned to the inside of the bra. Note: it does not matter which side you select; it is purely an aesthetic choice.

3. Set your machine.

The first pass of elastic attachment uses a regular zigzag stitch. The stitch width should be less than half the width of the elastic. For a ½" wide elastic, this means the zigzag would be less than ¼" wide.

4. Position elastic.

Place the elastic soft side up on the right side of the bra with the smooth edge of the elastic aligned with the edge of the fabric.

5. Sew first pass.

Stitch without stretching the elastic, placing your zigzag stitches as close as possible to the pi-cot edge without going over it. If you stitch over the right edge of the elastic two things happen: one, you will distort the look of the visible edge of the elastic in the final bra and two, it will lead to puckers in the fabric when you turn the elastic. Also, if your stitching is too far away from the right edge, when you turn the elastic you will see the unattractive rough side of the elastic.

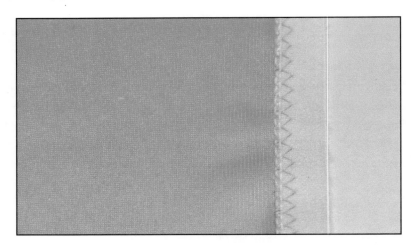

If at any point you did not get as close as necessary to the visible edge of the elastic, you can sew a small 1.5mm straight stitch up against the edge in that area only. This solution should not really be applied for lengths greater than ¼". The other option is to go back and re-stitch the area with the same zigzag, getting closer to the visible edge trim line.

As a rule, you do not stretch the elastic as you sew it to the bra. To understand why, it helps to know that its role is to keep the bra, which is already fitted, snug against the body. If you were to stretch the elastic while sewing, you would get a rippled-looking bra that is destined for a short life since the elastic will get more stretched out with each wearing of the bra.

There are two areas where the no stretch rule is broken: the underarm area and below the cups of a full frame bra. In these areas, use only the slightest of stretches, just enough to facilitate the turn of the elastic over these curves.

Pro tip: For symmetry under the cups on a full frame bra, mark the elastic turn points at the base of the cups. When you attach the elastic to the bottom of the frame, use these marks to align the picot edge of the elastic rather than lining up the smooth edge with the band. Following this marking when applying the elastic will help ensure that you have an equal amount of band under each cup when you turn the elastic to the wrong side.

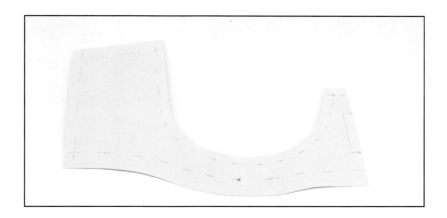

Pro tip: Consider your strap attachment when you are putting on the underarm elastic. If you are using a ring or slider attachment, you want to include the stabilizer in the elastic attachment process. See Straps section for details.

6. Trim fabric for flatness.

After you have completed sewing the first pass, trim the excess bra fabric beyond the stitching line and clip any curves right up to the

stitching. This keeps the bra and elastic flat without any pulls or wrinkles when turned to the inside of the bra.

> Pro tip: Do not cut the ends of the elastic until you have turned the elastic to the inside and sewn the 3-step zigzag! You want to be sure you have the correct length of elastic and a premature snip could make the elastic too short when it is turned to the inside of outwardly curving pieces.

7. Sew second pass.

To finish sewing the elastic, turn the elastic to the inside of the bra. Sew the elastic using a 3-step zigzag or serpentine stitch along the smooth edge of the elastic with the elastic side (soft side) up, again placing your stitching as close to the edge of the elastic as possible without going over the edge.

As you sew, be sure the bra is flat underneath the elastic by pulling slightly on the fabric in the opposite direction of the elastic as you sew. You may want to sew more slowly over slippery fabrics since they really want to shift as you stitch.

Now I know the right side of the fabric is on the machine bed. If you are worried about this, test the procedure first on a scrap of fabric. You sew with the elastic side up so you can be sure you are securing the entire span of elastic to the bra. If you were to sew on the elastic away from the edge, it could curl over on itself when you go to wear the bra creating a ridge that would be visible from the right side of the bra.

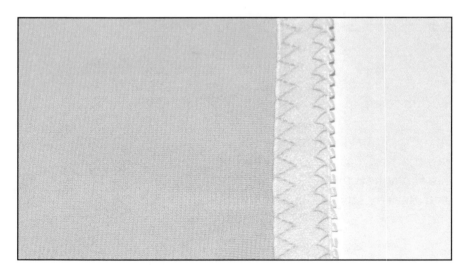

ATTACHING UNDERWIRE CASING

This is arguably the most challenging aspect of sewing bras. Like any sewing technique, after practicing it a few times you should have no problems. While there are acceptable alternative ways to seal up the wire casing, I always conceal the raw edge of the underwire casing at the arm side of the bra underneath the underarm elastic. The sequence of the following instructions reflects that technique. If you wish, you could seal the channel in an alternative fashion such as sealing it on top of the underarm elastic.

1. Adjust and test your machine settings.

To get started, the first thing you need to do is change your needle to an 80/12 Universal. This needle does a better job than the stretch needle in penetrating the casing. The second thing you need to do is test the machine tension when sewing on casing through the layers of fabric, anywhere from 2 to 4 layers depending on the location around the cup.

2. Measure casing.

To measure out the length of casing needed for each cup, lay it along the cup to frame seam line where it will be attached. I leave a tail of about 1" at the center front and underarm to help with handling during sewing and wire insertion.

3. Sew casing.

Casing is sewn to the cup with the plush side up. It is slightly stretched as it is sewn to the cup to frame seam allowance so you will not use pins. On the casing itself you can see a line where the wire channel begins and ends (see Supplies section for a detailed view of underwire casing). You will sew along this stitch line. If your casing has any curvature — it will be pretty clear if you lay it down flat on a table - you will want to be sure that it follows the curvature of the cup.

If you are making a full frame bra, the casing will be turned over the cup to frame seam allowance toward the frame. This means you attach the casing to the cup side of this seam allowance.

If you are making a frameless bra, the casing will be turned over the cup to frame seam allowance toward the cup. This means you attach the casing to the bridge/band side of the cup to frame seam allowance.

Line up the stitching line on the casing with the cup to frame seam line and sew around the cup. To start the line of stitching, put the needle through all the layers — casing and underlying seam allowance- and lift up the presser foot and be sure the needle is right on the line of stitching. Look for an alignment cue so you can align the stitching along the entire seam.

You can start sewing at either the underarm or at the center front. At the center front, you will sew the casing all the way to the top of the finished upper cup. At the underarm, you will sew only to a point that equals the width of your underarm elastic times two. So if you are using ⅜" elastic for the underarm, stop sewing the casing at ¾" (⅜" x 2) away from the underarm. This will make it easier to get the casing out of the way when you sew the first pass of underarm elastic, and make it easier to sew the casing closed before the second pass of the elastic attachment.

If the underwire casing attachment seam is not on top of or right up against the cup to frame seam, you need to fix it. You may think this is a small thing but it will absolutely haunt you when it comes time to pin stitch and topstitch the wire casing on the right side of the bra. If you don't fix the casing position now, you could easily end up obstructing the wire casing with the topstitching.

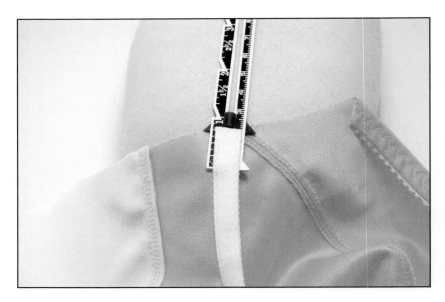

4. Trim seam allowance.

In our quest for a smooth garment that lies flat against the body, we want to eliminate bulk at every point of the construction process and this means trimming the seam allowance that will be underneath the casing.

5. Sew first pass of underarm elastic.

After the casing is attached, you will change the needle back to the Stretch needle and change your tension setting back to what you were using for sewing on the elastic and attach the underarm elastic — first pass of regular zigzag only. See the Attaching Lingerie Elastic section for details on this technique. You will need to move the wire casing out the way when you sew in the underarm area.

6. Seal the wire casing at the underarm.

You will end up concealing the sealed end of the underwire casing underneath the elastic in the second pass of elastic stitching, but first you need to properly close the wire casing.

First, mark the area of the casing that will be under the elastic by folding down the elastic behind the casing. Start by marking where the bottom of the elastic hits on the casing. Also mark where the lowest part of the zigzag stitching hits the casing for the next step. It is between these marks that you will sew the casing closed.

Next, change the machine needle back to the 80/12 Universal and sew the casing closed us-ing multiple rows of closely spaced straight stitches to get the casing nice and flat in the area that will be underneath the elastic.

7. Trim casing to fit under elastic.

You will likely need to cut the casing so it fits under the elastic when the elastic is turned to the inside of the bra. The cutting mark on the casing corresponds to where the first pass of zigzag stitching from the underarm elastic hits the casing.

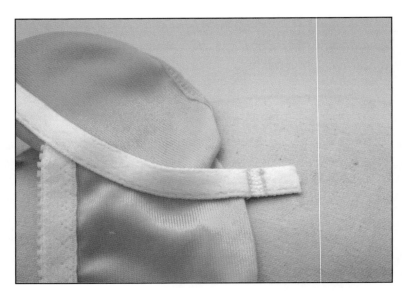

8. Finish the elastic.

Change back to the Stretch needle and reset the machine for sewing the second pass of elastic. Now you can trim the excess fabric along the first pass of elastic stitching, clip the curves and sew the second pass of the elastic.

9. Topstitch the wire casing.

If you have attached the casing properly along the cup to frame seam line, you will not have any problems at all with topstitching. First, change the needle back to the Universal and change the tension to what you were using for attaching the wire casing.

You will sew two lines of topstitching. The first is a line of pin stitching which will line up with the original casing attachment stitching from step 3 above. The second line will match up the casing stitching line on the opposite side of the casing.

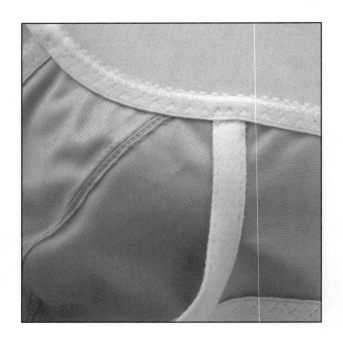

Topstitch with the right side of the bra facing up for the best looking top stitching on the front facing side of the bra. If you attached the casing properly in the first place you should not have any issues lining up your topstitching lines with the stitching lines of the casing. Provided you don't sew the casing closed when topstitching, it is ok if you are little bit off the stitching lines on the casing. No one will know but you.

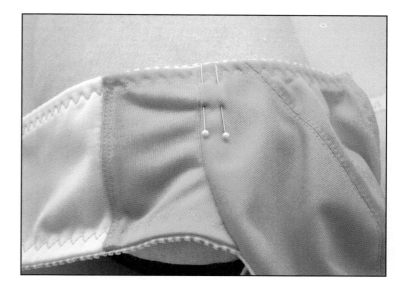

Pro tip: Thread match your top and bottom thread color to the area you are sewing on for an interior that looks as nice as the exterior. It also helps disguise any slight deviation from the wire casing stitching line that may happen during the topstitching process.

First sew the pin stitch row. You want to just hold the cup (frameless) or band (full frame) taut as you stitch. After topstitching, look at the casing side. How did you do? Can you still fit a wire through the casing? Are you on the stitching line of the casing? I would only adjust the topstitching if the casing was closed as a result of the topstitching, or other fabric was caught up in the stitching.

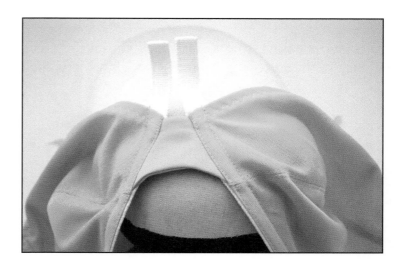

The second row of stitching will be on the stitching line on the opposite side of the casing. Measure this so you know how far away it is from the pin stitching. When you are ready to stitch, put the needle through all the layers and lift the presser foot with the needle still in the down position to check your placement. Adjust as necessary and look for a visual cue to maintain this throughout your topstitching.

Again, after stitching check the casing side. Did you secure the casing to the bra all the way around? The casing must be secured, so you need to re-stitch any loose areas. Is the casing still open enough to hold a wire? If not, you will need to fix it.

Pro tip: **Pro tip:** Write down your machine settings, needle positions and presser foot guides for each construction technique so you can refer back to them. Once you have them figured out, it will speed up your process.

10. Insert underwires and seal the wire casing at the center front.

Once the bra is complete but still flat (the straps have not yet been connected front to back), close the wire casing. You could save closing the casing until just prior to attaching the center embellishment but I prefer working with a flat bra without its underwire for as long as possible.

To seal the casing, first insert the wire. Note: the colored tip of the wire is intended to be at the center front. See the section on Cutting Underwires Down to Size if your wire is too long. If your wire is too short, you must find longer wires. Shorter wires will not work.

Once the wire is inserted, push it all the way to the underarm closure. This gives you the most room possible to seal the casing without risking breaking a needle on the wire.

Be sure you have the Universal needle in and the tension at the setting used to attach the casing. Traditionally a bar tack is used to seal the casing but like the control, look and flatness I get by sewing a small box using a straight stitch. I use the height of the 3-step zigzag from the upper cup trim – or other marker on the trim if you used something else - for my stitching box. The width of the box equals the width of the casing.

11. Trim and seal.

Once the casing is closed, you can trim the excess casing, being very careful to cut the casing only. I cut the casing at an angle so the plush backing does not show from the right side. I do keep casing all the way up to the very top of the upper cup for a smooth line all the way around the cup.

12. Once the bra is complete, treat the cut edges of the casing with Fray Check and allow to dry.

SIDE BONING

There are times when you will want to add additional support to the band of the bra. One option for doing so is to add boning to the side seams. This technique is only recommended for bras that are designed with a side seam.

This application of side boning differs from the underwire casing application in that it is not stretched as it is applied and neither end is concealed under the elastics of the bra. The omission of concealment allows the boning to span a greater distance and provides for a smooth and balanced appearance at the underarm.

1. Sew the side seam of the bra. Do not topstitch or trim the seam allowance.

2. Measure the side seam of the bra and cut a length of underwire casing or boning casing this length, plus 1" to 2" to make it easier to get the casing out the way when you are sewing the elastics onto the band.

3. Change your machine to a Universal needle and increase machine tension. Sew one side of the casing onto the band side of the side seam allowance using a straight stitch. Do not stretch the casing as you sew it. Just like sewing underwire casing, sew through the casing right on top of the side seam line.

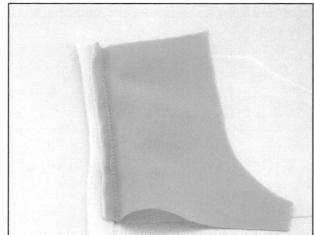

At each edge of the band, stop stitching the casing at a distance equal to two times your elastic. For example, if the band elastic is ½," stop sewing 1" from the bottom of the side seam.

4. Proceed with bra construction as usual, moving the boning casing out of the way when you sew elastics to the band. You will not topstitch or seal the casing until just prior to inserting the underwires into the bra.

5. When you are ready to complete the boning casing, start by topstitching through the bra and casing from the right side of the frame. Change to a Universal needle and increase your tension to make two lines of stitching, one row of pin stitching along the side seam and another row that catches the opposite edge of the boning casing underneath. Sew these lines from the top to the bottom of the band.

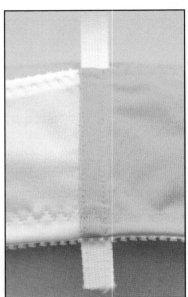

6. Seal one side of the boning casing by sewing a bar tack through all layers: the frame, elastic and boning casing. Trim the excess casing from the sealed side.

7. Measure the length of boning needed. Boning will extend from the casing closure you made in the previous step to where you will seal the casing on the other side of the band, less some room for the boning to move around so it does not push through the casing when it is under stress. To find this length, measure from the sealed side of the casing to opposite edge of the band. Subtract ¼" for the boning to move around and another ⅛" for sealing the casing.

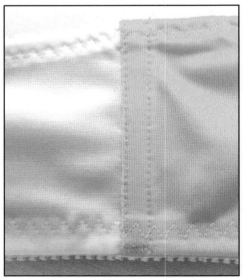

8. Insert the boning into the casing, pressing it all the way down to the sealed side. Now seal the boning inside the casing using a bar tack sewn through all layers: the frame, elastic and boning casing. Trim the excess casing.

9. Once the bra is complete, treat the cut edges of the casing with Fray Check and allow to dry.

STRAPS

There are more bra strap style variations than I can cover here but I will cover the attachments that I use most frequently. Many of the techniques can be applied to whatever strap treatment you are working with.

Since the front of the straps are an integral part of the bra design, your pattern will dictate the fabrication and attachment process. Keep in mind that you want the portion of the strap that goes over the shoulder to have little to no movement, especially if your cup size is a C or greater. If you are using fabric with movement, it should be stabilized to remove as much of it as possible.

The backs of the straps are usually a separate elasticized piece so that the body can move comfortably. While you could make the straps a set length — this is custom after all - they should be adjustable so you can shorten them as the straps starts to lose their elasticity.

Front Straps

My favorite front strap treatment is to thread the strap through a ring that is attached to the top of the bra. If you want to apply your straps this way, you will need to prep for this treatment during the sewing of the underarm elastic. Specifically, you need to apply stabilizer to the portion of the elastic that will be folded back on it to hold the ring. If you don't do this, the elastic will get all stretched out in this area pretty quickly and wavy elastic is not attractive.

1. When measuring for underarm elastic, allow for an additional 1" at the front of the bra for folding back over the ring.

2. Cut stabilizer to match the width of the elastic.

3. Measure stabilizer.

The stabilizer should be no longer than the amount of the elastic that will be turned back to hold the ring. If it is longer, the stabilizer will extend into the plush area of the elastic and it may rub and irritate the skin in the underarm area.

4. Attach stabilizer.

Sew the stabilizer to the plush side of the elastic during the first pass of zigzag stitching on the elastic. It is attached to the plush side because otherwise it would be visible when the elastic was turned and folded over the ring. Be sure to continue your stitching up through the excess elastic at the top of the upper cup to catch the stabilizer.

5. Finish elastic attachment.

Complete the second pass on the elastic as usual. Again, extend your stitching the entire way up through the excess elastic at the top of the cup. I recommend separately stitching the stabilized piece of elastic to enclose the ring after you have attached the underarm elastic. You need more than a 3-step zigzag to secure the ring and it is far easier to get symmetrical strap attachments this way.

6. Fold elastic over the ring to the wrong side of the bra.

You can use your judgment on the fold back in terms of how much of the wrong side of the elastic is showing, but I like to minimize it. Once I fold back one side, I fold the other side to match for symmetrical strap attachments.

7. Secure ring.

To secure the elastic holding the ring, I use a straight stitch and sew a small box. It gives more control than a bar tack and helps keep the area flat with barely visible stitches.

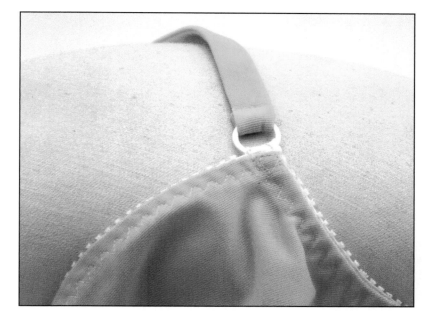

When you are ready, you can attach the front strap to the rings by threading it through the ring and stitching two straight rows across the entire width of the strap to secure.

Back Straps

The back straps are elastic with an adjustment mechanism – a ring and a slider - so they can be adjusted as they lose their elasticity over time. While assembled versions are available, it is easy to make your own.

To assemble the back straps:

1. Place the elastic shiny side up and thread it over the center bar of the slider.

2. Pull just enough elastic through the slider to stitch the elastic to the wrong side of the strap.

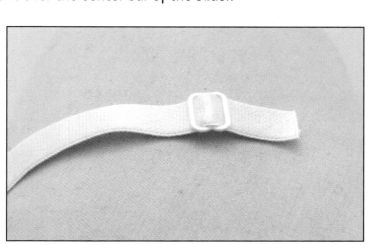

3. On the right side of the elastic using a zipper foot and a straight stitch, secure the slider to the elastic, getting as close as possible to the slider.

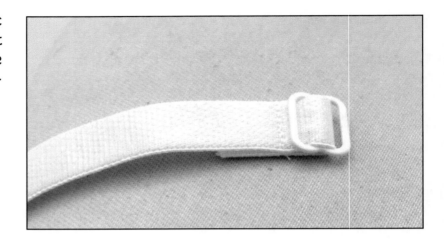

4. Thread the elastic through a ring. This ring is where your front strap will be attached. You can also use another slider, but if you do that, be sure to thread only through one side bar. You need to leave a bar free for the front strap to fit through.

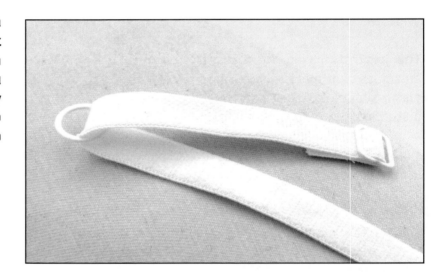

5. Thread the elastic back through the slider by going under the outermost bars and over the center bar, following where you threaded the elastic through in step 1. It will be a tight squeeze to get it through but that is what we are looking for. When you adjust your strap to be a certain !ength for wearing, you do not want it to move easily.

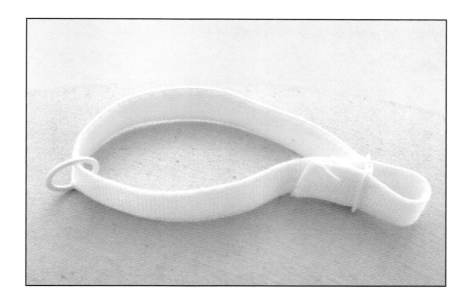

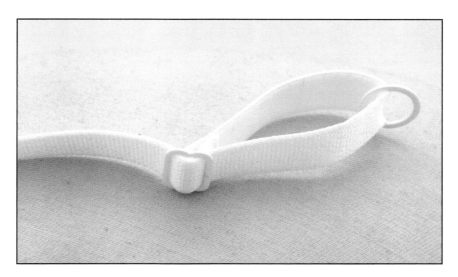

Pro tip: **Some strap elastics have directionality. That is, they have a slight curve. Check this before you make the straps, so you can make a left curving strap for the left side of the bra and a right curving strap for the right side. To determine any curvature, lay your elastic right side up on a flat surface. In the following picture, the straps on the left curve up to the right and would be placed on the right side of the back of the bra. The straps on the right curve up to the left and would be placed on the left side of the back of the bra.**

ATTACHING BACK STRAPS

Bra back styles vary so I am going to cover the two most frequent back strap attachments for the most common bra back styles that I use: the Scoop Back and the T Back. If your bra back has a Scoop Back, you will not attach the straps until all the other elastics have been attached. For the T Back, the strap attachment can be combined with the band elastic attachment or attached directly to the band elastics at the end of the construction process.

Scoop Back Band

1. Check the height of the back closure.

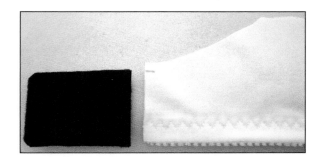

Before you stitch the strap elastic to the bra, be sure that the height of the back corresponds to the height of your hook and eye closure. To find out if the final height is correct, lay the eye piece of the back fastener on top of the left side of the bra back to see if the edges of the eye piece will just enclose this area.

If the back is too high, mark the excess fabric visible above the fastener. This mark is where you will align the upper edge of the strap elastic when you attach it to the scoop.

If the back is too low and the eye piece is on its own with no bra feeding into it, then you will need to lay the strap elastic on the area and maneuver it until you have the upper edge of the elastic aligned with the top of the closure. Once you have found this position, mark the bottom edge of the elastic on the back of the bra. This is where you will align the elastic when you attach it to the bra.

Repeat this process for the hook side of the bra back. (Note the hook side of the bra was used above for illustrative purposes only, the eyes are attached to the left side of the bra.)

2. Attach back strap.

To attach the strap to the bra, line up the elastic with the scoop in the back of the bra, or your markings if you adjusted for height. If your elastic has directionality, be sure you are attaching the strap to the correct side of the back. Sew the strap to the bra using a very small zigzag stitch, first in the center of the strap. Follow that by sewing another line of stitching on the side of the elastic on the most interior side of the bra, without stretching the elastic. Sewing is done from the right side of the elastic.

3. Trim excess fabric.

In the interest of eliminating bulk, trim the bra behind the elastic up to the center line of stitching. Also trim the strap elastic so it is flush with the back of the bra where the hook or eye closure will be attached.

T Back Band

Applying straps to a T Back band can be as simple as sewing the back straps on top of the elastics at the upper and lower band, or as involved as concealing the end of the back elastic underneath the band elastic. As with many parts of bra construction, you have options.

If you are attaching the back strap by sewing on top of the band and underarm elastics, you just sew a bar tack through the bra, elastic and the entire width of the strap, bra side up. Be sure to do this at both the bottom and the top of the band. This approach has the advantage of allowing you to determine the back strap placement after you have tried the bra on and it makes moving the straps fairly easy.

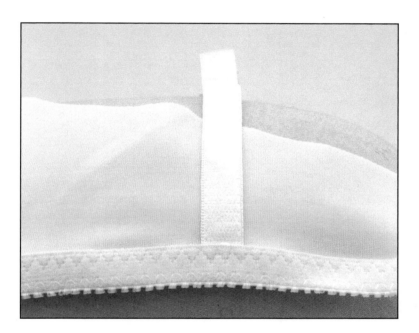

If you want to conceal the bottom edge of the elastic under the band elastic, you need to plan your back strap placement in advance and make your straps in advance so they are ready to be caught under the second pass of elastic stitching of the band elastic. Be sure to also sew a bar tack through the bra, elastic and the entire width of the strap at the top of the band.

HOOK AND EYE CLOSURE

The back closure can be a challenging area to get professional looking results, especially on the hook side since the hooks cannot be laid on the machine bed for attachment. Perhaps for this reason, I like to start with the easier side— the eye side.

Eyes

The eyes of the bra go on the left hand side of the back of the bra.

1. Position eyes.

Open the eye attachment all the way. It will open up to the line of stitching by the back row of eyes. Insert the back of the bra into the opening.

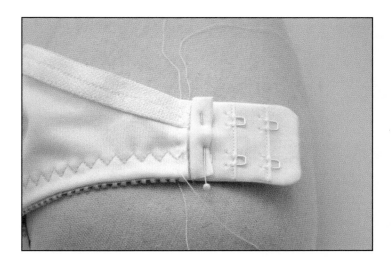

2. Baste and align.

Fold back the top (right side) of the eyes and baste a row of stitching between the end and the back row of eyes to facilitate handling. Next, with the top still folded back, baste a line of stitching or use pins to mark where the eye piece ends on the bra.

Now, fold down the top flap and match it up with where you marked the end of the eye piece. Also check the sides of the eye piece and line them up there to ensure you catch all the layers in the final stitching.

3. **Sew.**

Once the eye piece layers are aligned, stitch the eye piece on and closed by starting at the line of stitching on the back row of eyes. If you cut your eyes from a roll, start at the top of the eye piece.

Sew close to the edge using a small straight stitch or small zigzag stitch. Sew to the back of the eye piece, across the back, and then up the other side to the stitching line and back row of hooks. Remove basting threads.

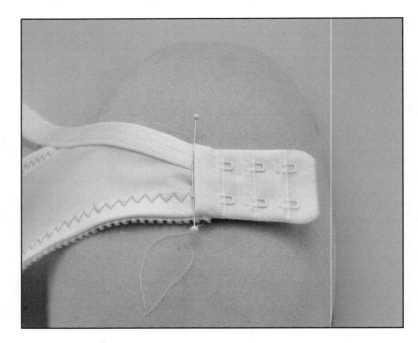

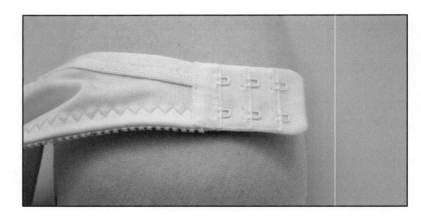

Hooks

The hooks of the bra go on the right hand side of the bra. The hooks are oriented toward the body. Remember you cannot put the hooks on the machine bed.

1. Position hooks.

Open the hook piece by unfolding it. To get the placement correct, note the position where the hooks fold and wrap easily around the back of the bra and align that point with the end of the bra.

2. Baste and align.

Hook side up; place the unfolded piece on the right side of the bra. Baste the piece to the bra somewhere in the center of the area between the hooks and the end of the hook piece.

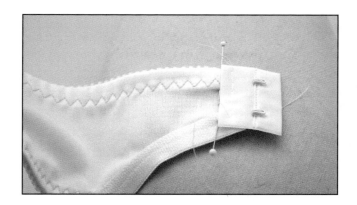

Sew another line of basting, or pin mark, where the very edge of the hook piece is. This will help you align the hook piece when folded.

3. Sew.

Fold the hook piece over the back of the bra into its final position. You are now working on the wrong side of the bra.

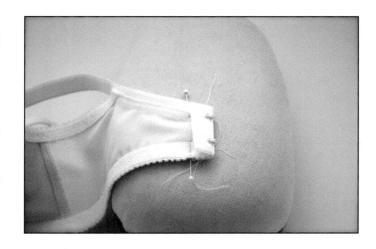

Secure the back edge of the hook piece into the correct position first. To do this, align the back of the hook piece with your basting or pin line that marks the edge of the hook piece on the front of the bra. Also, check the sides of the hook piece and line them up there to ensure you will be able to catch all the layers in the final stitching.

Sew using a small straight stitch or small zigzag stitch close to the edge through all layers, including the top and bottom layers of the closure and the bra fabric. You may need to use a zipper foot do to this.

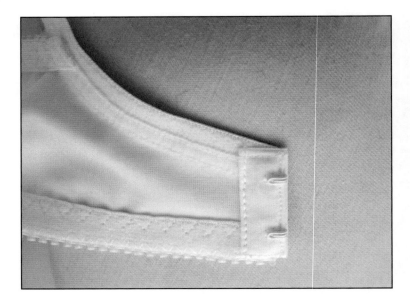

Luckily, you will see that there are subtle vertical lines running through the hook piece. You can use one of these lines as your stitching guide — provided that the lines are straight up and down on your supplies.

Now you can sew the sides of the eye piece closed. Again, stitch as close to the edges as possible in order to catch both top and bottom layers of the closure, using a zipper foot if necessary.

ATTACHING BOW/CENTERPIECE DECORATION

While purely optional, I like to attach an embellishment to the center font of the bra since bras without decoration always seem a bit unfinished to me. Since using a sewing machine is difficult, if not impossible in this area, the embellishment is attached by hand.

The only note here is to be sure that you are attaching the decoration so that it is securely attached and does not twist or lift off the bra awkwardly.

CUTTING UNDERWIRES
DOWN TO SIZE

Depending on the style, your underwires may be too long to fit into the bra. It is actually fairly simple to cut them to the desired size.

I always close my wires from the center front, which is a good idea if your wire is too long. Generally, the height of the center front is the reason your wire is too long, so this is the side where you will mark and cut your wire.

To cut underwires, first measure the finished wire length you want.

1. Insert the wire into casing that has been top stitched to its final place and remains open on only one side.

2. Insert the wire all the way to the stitches sealing the wire casing on the closed side.

3. With the wire inserted, mark the wire at the very edge of the bra taking care not to get any marker on the bra itself, and then remove the wire. This only gives you the total length of the channel; this is not where you cut the wire.

4. Measure down from your mark in step 3 by a "wire play" allowance so the wire does not burst through the casing under the wearing pressure when the wire is splayed. Allow ⅛" of space for each side of the wire, for a total of ¼" (⅛" + ⅛" = ¼"). Measure down ¼" from your marking in step 3.

5. Measure down from your mark in step 4 by a stitching allowance to close the casing. Use the width of your trim for your stitching allowance. For example, if the trim is ⅜", I add ⅜" stitching room. If you have no trim, measure down by ⅜." This marking, a total of ⅝" (¼" + ⅜") down from your original marking, is where you will cut the wire.

The easiest way to cut the wire is to use a wire cutter. I recommend putting on protective eyewear and putting the wire into a vise first to hold it stationary and allow you to have both hands free. You do not want any stray bits of wire to land in your eye. Cut the wires one at a time.

Once the wire is cut, you need to seal the rough edges. I use Household Goop. Just take care to not use too much so you don't end up with a bulky knob at the end the wire.

BENDING UNDERWIRES

Sometimes you want a differently shaped wire. Perhaps you are trying to match the curvature of a ready-to-wear bra. You can bend the wires, within reason, to fit your body.

You may also wish to bend an underwire for comfort. If you place an underwire on the table, you can see that it is flat. The chest wall beneath the breast is not always flat so you may need to bend the wire a bit so it will rest more comfortably on the body. You only need a slight and gentle bend to shape the wire. Once wires are bent, they do not go back to their original shape so don't over do it!

To bend wires, first mark the point of the wire that will be at the base of the breast. For a full frame bra, you can find this point by holding your wire up to your frame pattern. For a frameless bra, you will need to lay the wire on the finished and installed wire casing.

Gently bend the wire around this base marking. Just put the spot you want to bend at the edge of a table. Hold the wire to the table with one hand while placing the palm of the other hand on top of the wire, just off the table. Press down on the wire to bend it. Three or four gentle bends is all it usually takes to contour the wire to the body.

REPLICATING YOUR SUCCESS

Once you make a beautiful and great fitting bra, you are going to want more. Therefore, here is some guidance on the best way to memorialize your successful pattern for future use and how to use it going forward.

First, you need to commit your pattern to oak tag or other light card stock. You need pattern pieces that can stand up to be being traced because going forward you will trace your pattern pieces onto your fabric and then cut away your tracing marks.

To trace the pattern pieces onto the fabric you can use chalk, a pen or a marker but not a wash out marker since they tend to bleed into the fabric. You need an accurate tracing line. No need to worry about whether your tracing marker will wash out since you will be cutting off the line you marked.

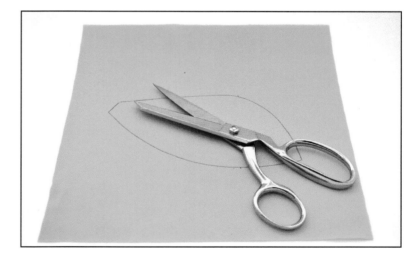

If you are tracing using a permanent marker, do not to use it for marking construction points. Either make a very small clip at the notch or use a washable marker, so you don't risk an unfortunate permanent spot in the final bra.

Another potential change from your normal operations is the way you will cut out your pattern. You should use your shears, not a rotary cutter. Shears give you far more control and accuracy, regardless of your rotary cutting skills.

Pro tip: **Do not try to use a rotary cutter to cut directly around the oak tag pieces. It does not matter how careful you are; you will shave off the edges of the pattern pieces. It seems harmless but over three or four bras, the pattern pieces shrink, changing the size and fit of the bra.**

A SHORT LESSON ON DYEING

If you find yourself unable to locate just the right color elastics and findings to go with your fabric, you can dye them to match. Elastics, wire casing and hook and eye closures all take wonderfully to dye. You can also dye fabrics. Natural fibers (cotton, silk, etc.) and nylon dye well, while polyester or fabrics with special coating do not.

I follow the RIT dye "sink and tub" instructions, adding as much dye liquid to hot water as necessary to get the color I want. A few tips when dyeing:

1. Dye fabric before you cut out the pieces, in case there are any unevenly colored spots.

2. Get the pieces to be dyed thoroughly wet before adding to the dye pot. If you don't, they won't take the dye evenly.

3. Be sure to test the dye on a scrap or swatch before adding your supplies. It can take a few tries to get the color you want.

4. Be sure to fully open up any fabric or elastic before putting it in the pot so you get even coloration. This also helps with even tinting.

5. Dye each type of object separately since each finding and fabric absorbs dye at a different rate. Things like strap elastic and underwire casing color quickly.

6. Once you add the objects to the pot, keep stirring them around for even dyeing and frequently check to see if they have reached your desired color.

7. Only work on a dyeing project in a well-lit place, preferably in daylight, so you can truly assess the color. Also keep in mind that colors look a little bit darker when wet.

8. When you take the item out of the dye pot, rinse thoroughly in running warm water.

9. Dye more than you need for the project, just in case! It is really hard to duplicate the same color mix. Better to have some extra left over then to not have enough.

FABRIC MANIPULATION

As frequently happens, we fall in love with a fabric that is unsuitable for our project. Luckily there are ways to make a fabric suitable for bra making.

If a fabric has too much stretch – the most common "flaw" - you may be able to make it work by doubling the fabric or by layering the fabric with one that has more desirable properties. Both approaches decrease the movement properties of the fabric. The only rule is that the top layer of fabric must contain equal or more movement than the base layer. There are three basic approaches to layering fabrics: putting two fabrics together, fusing fabric to a stretch tricot interfacing, or lining the fabric.

The most common fabric manipulation in my studio is layering a stretch lace over a tricot or power net for a lacy looking bra that provides great support. The easiest way to connect the two layers of fabric together for easier handling during construction is to use spray adhesive.

To create an overlay, first cut a piece of the overlay fabric in a rough rectangle larger than the cut pattern piece you are going to cover. Take care to make sure that the direction of greatest stretch matches the pattern. Next, spray the right or outward facing base layer of fabric with the adhesive following the adhesive maker's instructions. Finally, adhere the rectangle of overlay fabric to the base fabric piece, making sure the overlay fabric is right side up and

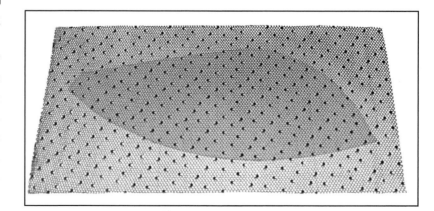

flat. Then trim away the excess overlay using the bra piece base layer as a guide. Now you can treat the two layers as one in the construction process.

If you are looking to use a non-lace fabric that has too much stretch, such as a four-way stretch jersey, you can bond the fabric to lightweight tricot interfacing to use for the frame and/or cups. In this case, cut the interfacing from the pattern and cut a rough rectangle of your fashion fabric slightly larger than the tricot piece. Bond the fabric to the interfacing following the manufacturer's instructions, then cut the fashion fabric using the interfacing piece as your guide. You have now created a new, more stable fabric to use in the bra. Note that you cannot use this bonded combination for the band since the stretch load will be too great.

A third approach to fabric manipulation is to line the fabric with a sheer nylon tricot. This approach works well under laces, fabrics that are uncomfortable against the skin, or fabrics that are close the stretch requirements for the bra. You will cut the same pieces as you cut for your fashion fabric; however, depending on how many pieces of the cup you are lining, you can be strategic about how you attach the lining to enclose seam allowances. As I cannot foresee how you will need to line the cup, I shall leave that strategy up to you!

AFTERWORD

I hope you have benefitted from this book and produced a bra that you proudly wear. If there are bra making topics you wish to learn about, please send me an email at info@orange-lingerie.com.

ABOUT THE AUTHOR

Norma Loehr spent her youth as an avid seamstress and designer but put it aside to focus on a career in finance. When she could not locate a luxury custom bra making service in North America, Norma left her position at a major Wall Street firm in New York to focus on the study and practice of custom bra making and founded Orange Lingerie. She is now based in Boston.

You can read more about Norma and see her work at http://www.orange-lingerie.com.

Printed in Great Britain
by Amazon.co.uk, Ltd.,
Marston Gate.